Record of Money Exchanges

Date and Place	Amount Dollars	Rate	Amount Received	Fees	For Whom (self, group, individual)

For more money information & research see page 34.

Publisher's Cataloging-in-Publication Data

Smithgall, Daryl.
    Short-Term Missions Participant
Handbook: Preparation & Field Guide.
    p. cm.
    ISBN 0-9777583-1-1
1. Short-Term Missions. 2. Christian Life.
I. Title.

BV2063.S__ 2006
266-dc21

Dedication

This book is dedicated to all those servants of Christ on both short-term and long-term missions who have been willing to "step out of the boat," take a risk, and make a difference around the world.

About the Author

Daryl Smithgall is the founder and executive director of Footsteps Missions and has led short-term missions in over 25 countries for projects of all types. Daryl has helped scores of churches, other organizations, and individuals prepare groups for short-term trips. He continues to lead several trips a year, and directs other Footsteps leaders. A recognized expert in the field, Daryl has written articles that appeared in major mission magazines and given talks before national organizations on short-term mission topics.

About Footsteps Missions

Footsteps Missions, a registered 501(c)(3) nonprofit corporation, assists individuals, churches and other organizations to conduct short-term missions. Footsteps provides a range of services that help the trip organizer. These include travel research for low-cost air fares and travel insurance for mission groups. Footsteps can perform part or all preparation for a trip, for example just pre-trip training or full trip organization and provision of trip leaders. Footsteps can support a trip serving a ministry or missionary that a group already has a relationship with, or, if needed, Footsteps has a network of partner ministries worldwide that allows trip organizers to find a good partner to work with in host countries. For more information, visit www.footstepsmissions.org.

Acknowledgements

This book is a collaborative effort of many short-term mission leaders and participants and, most importantly, host country ministry partners, who, when we stopped and listened, told us what worked and what didn't work.

The book's editor and a significant contributor of content is Phil Kiekhaefer, Ph.D., a trip participant, leader, and former Peace Corps volunteer. Layout and graphics by dystrick design, Inc., with special thanks to Josephine Voong for design of forms, tables and worksheets and Joe Couto for the cover design. Some illustrations are by Jeanette Munter. Researchers included

Emily Schreiber and Dennis Smithgall. Major contributions for several chapters were completed by Shaun Sheahan. Other contributors included Steve Bander, M.D.; Darrah Garvin, Ph.D.; Ed Bauman, Meg Roundy, and Eileen Clark.

As the primary author and director of Footsteps Missions, I want to thank all of those named above and countless others who have touched our hearts and taught us the knowledge and understanding we have worked to include in this book. We hope this book helps make your next mission more successful.

— Daryl Smithgall

Have a Suggestion for the Next Edition?

If you have a suggestion for the next edition please submit it to books@footstepsmissions.org. For copyright and publication purposes, all submissions become property of Footsteps Missions.

Disclaimer

The author and contributors have made every effort that the information in this book is accurate but neither they nor the publishers nor anyone else connected with this book's production assume responsibility for the services of any business named or otherwise indicated in this book; for any errors or omissions; or for any loss, damage, or disruptions to you for any reason involving use of the information, advice, or recommendations in this book.

Introduction

If you are planning to go on a short-term mission, this book is designed for you. Whether you've been on a trip before or this will be your first, this book can help you get ready before the trip and enrich your experience while on the trip and afterward. This book is written for the trip participant who is not the group leader. Footsteps publishes a different book for the organizer or leader of the trip (*The Footsteps Short-Term Missions Leadership Handbook,* ISBN #0-9777583-0-3).

This short-term mission participant handbook is the product of several hundred mission trips, countless successful projects, and countless moments when someone has said, "Oops! Well, I won't do that next time" or "I wish I had done this before I left," or "If only I had brought my friends' addresses." For many participants, a mission trip is a once-in-a-lifetime or rare event, with few second chances to learn from a bad experience. Our experience can help you avoid common short-term mission mistakes and clear the way for a successful trip.

Use this book to prepare

This book helps you get ready and check off that the right arrangements have been made. As you use this book, fill in the information for your trip. The book is, in part, a research coach to help you gather the information you'll need. It is also part checklist so you don't forget the essential things you need to do.

Use this book on the trip

This book provides a field tool for when you are in the host country. Its tools help you collect your thoughts and make the most of your experience by engaging with it. Finally, it is a reference, with handy and sometimes crucial information you may need in the host country.

Suggest that your trip leader use the companion book

As mentioned above, for group leaders, Footsteps Missions has a companion book to this participant guide. To order, email us at books@footstepsmissions or visit our website at www.footstepsmissions.org.

Table of Contents

Short-Term
"Mission Statements"

1. Smiles are a universal language

2. It's camping with a purpose

3. Meaning-Full!

4. My home seems different, richer spiritually somehow, because I shared the lives of those we met

5. I still wake up hoping there will be fried bread and warm milk with the cream left in it ready for me, like there was on the trip

6. Never been so tired, so sore, so happy

7. We saw the changing of the hearts

8. We didn't do what we thought we'd do—thankfully! We did something much better.

9. I didn't think I could... and then we did...

10. What will be your mission statement?

_____

The Servant of All: Going to Serve on a Short-Term Mission

In John 13:1, we are told that Jesus is about to show the disciples "the full extent of His love." Jesus then takes a basin of water and a towel and bends down below the eye level of each disciple and... well... washes their feet. Jesus explains this show of love by saying, "I am the Lord and I have washed your feet."

What an odd thing to say, if we think about it. They already know he is the Lord, *and* what he just did. It is as if he must remind the shocked disciples he is still who he is—that performing this humble service has not diminished his status as Lord one bit. By showing that *the Lord* can wash their feet, he forces the disciples to rethink their ideas about what is beneath them to do, ideas that could stop them from conveying Jesus' love to others, as he just did. The message is clear: if the Lord can serve others humbly, you can too.

All this, Jesus conveys with a simple example. Likewise, your example can convey Jesus' love. Your willingness to "wash feet" can motivate others to Christ. Going on a short-term mission can be about a lot of things. It can be about the excitement of traveling to a foreign country. It can be about making new friends, both in the host country and among your mission team. It can be about learning new things about yourself, your capabilities, your talents, your spiritual nature. But at the heart of a short-term mission is the willingness to serve, to be a servant.

Short-term mission trips can be wonderful, wonderful experiences for the participants and host country ministries. Great things happen and Christ's love abounds in the most unexpected ways. Short-term missions have built churches and schools, dug wells, put on vacation Bible schools, taught English, provided medical care, and too many things to list that are good, positive, and successful. In contrast, a book like this sometimes focuses on the negatives much more than we hope your mission trip will warrant.

We hope that by giving you some instances to avoid, your trip will succeed. Most do. More would succeed or improve with a little forewarning, as we provide here and throughout the book. In this spirit, we hope you read through the following and take the lessons of our experience to heart for yourself.

What Ruins Short-Term Mission Trips

A short-term mission can be a wonderful growing experience for those who serve, as well as for those who are being served. On the negative side, trips can compromise and even set back ministry. When I ask missionaries and partners around the world their perspective on what destroys a short-term ministry, three major themes keep coming up:

- Lack of preparation
- Cultural insensitivity
- People who insist on meeting perceived needs, not "real" needs

What are real needs? It is far better to do a simple service truly needed, such as picking up garbage or painting a room, than to force a well-intentioned project that doesn't fit the culture, meets a need that the locals don't see as a priority, or meets a need the locals don't see as a need at all. A related issue is the "gold-plated toaster" gift. If you need a new kitchen and someone gives you a gold-plated toaster, you will likely accept it with a thank you, but it's not meeting your real needs.

Let's look at an example. Hearing of water problems, a group might plan to build a concrete cistern to hold rainwater. In country, the group listens and discovers the real water issue is trash in a reservoir. While less glamorous than the construction of the smaller-impact, "gold-plated" gift, the group's time is best spent hauling trash from the reservoir.

Your group as a whole will have to determine what needs you will meet in your choice of your service project. As a team member, you can be aware of what to watch for and be supportive of changes in plans to meet a host partner's real needs. It may mean giving up that idea of directing a crew mixing concrete and instead stepping into some murky water to pull out trash. Those tools you carefully collected and packed may never leave their boxes.

It isn't always clear where you should step next in a mission trip—are you wading toward success by entering those murky waters or are you stepping into trouble? Each of the following seven landmines have been exploded by many an unwary mission trip participant. Watch where you step!

1. Lack of Preparation

If you find yourself planning and prepping on the flight to your destination, you are too late. If you prepare beforehand, you will feel more relaxed and ready. If your group has orientation meetings, attend them. If your group has service training, attend it. Are you comfortable with the technical knowledge you will need for your project? If not, there are likely ways you can work on learning more or practicing before getting in country.

Spend some time with the exercises in this book to learn about the country you will visit. Also spend time preparing your testimony with the tools in the book. Make time to visit the local library and check out a book about the country, region, or people you will be working with. Check "Google News" for news about your country every so often before your departure date. If you can, read the news as written by host country publications. Most important, spend some time with your thoughts and in prayer regarding why you are going on the mission and what you hope to accomplish.

2. Cultural Insensitivity

You've probably heard the term "the Ugly American." The image is of a loud, arrogant, pushy, bossy American dressed in garb that wouldn't be appropriate in any setting, shouting commands or opinions that would embarrass the most courageous of us. These folks show up at the most sensitive of times and can ruin relationships with our host country partners. Sometimes the ugliness can be subtle, for example intimating that your (American) way of doing things is the right way and the locals should just defer to your knowledge on the subject.

The key to avoiding the ugly American role is to be a student of the culture and to build partnerships with the locals that allow you to work in tandem, problem solving how you can help in *their* community. This book's "Learning Your Host Country's Culture" section will help you be a student of the culture, and throughout this book, we give you ways to serve your partners respectfully.

3. Public Displays of Affection (PDAs)

A kiss is not just a kiss, when it's insulting to your hosts. This issue falls into the cultural sensitivity category but merits its own listing. PDAs provoke strong negative reactions in many other cultures. Hugging, kissing, touching, or flirtatious talk that you might consider common behavior might be deeply offensive. Conservative behavior regarding physical or intimate relations is wise—within your group and in relations with host country people.

4. Not Giving Your Best

When you give your best, you value and respect those who are receiving you. Many a short-term missionary has had an attitude of giving leftovers: "Oh they're poor—they'll like anything we do; we don't really need to prepare much." That's not giving your first fruits. Your host country partners can tell the difference right away.

5. Romance

Exotic locales, new people, excitement! This can spell Club Trouble on a mission trip. Consider the trip off limits for anything more than friendships to develop (there is too much at stake to take this lightly). If you find someone with whom you think you will click romantically, hold off acting on that part of the relationship during the trip. Develop that part of the relationship after the trip or on a separate trip not involving a mission component. A base of friendship and experience of shared service can be the foundation of a rewarding romantic relationship—later.

6. Weak Boundaries

An unmarried woman within the group may attract a male from the host country without meaning too. The woman's reaction to the extra attention given her can be a no-win situation. If she remains nice, not wanting to hurt feelings, she could inadvertently encourage him. If she ignores him, this could be seen as rude. This example could be played out with a male visitor too. Finding appropriate, tactful boundaries is a must, and even distancing yourself from someone may be necessary.

7. Creating Dependency

Creating dependency is a form of not meeting the host ministry's real needs. All ministries have a real need to be self-sustaining. Successful service stimulates inspiration and partnership rather than fostering dependency on the next group that comes along. Let's imagine that a short-term mission group shows up at the host church and finds, besides the building needing paint, that the roof is in horrible shape and the bathrooms... well... what bathrooms? So that week they paint, do a VBS (vacation Bible school), do a special evening service, add the roof project to their list, build a bathroom, and finally leave the host church with a generous monetary offering.

These short-termers went home feeling great because of all they had accomplished. The host church was left feeling great because of all that the generous group had done, but they were also left WAITING for these short-termers or others like them to come back and solve whatever was left and whatever came up after the group left. This church is dependent, not inspired. Sometimes the best ministry leaves something undone. It leaves the team feeling incomplete but helps the church to mobilize and finish the task.

As short-term missionaries, our goal is to have a partnership, to come *alongside* and enable the host church, ministers, or community to act. That may mean that the short-termer provides materials for a project, but the hosts provide the labor—that kind of partnership can produce ownership and inspiration for the hosts, allowing them to be interdependent and motivated for His Kingdom work. Leaving a house unfinished may give the owners a chance to finish it. They can take ownership rather than acquiring a gift that they value less because it involved no effort. Doing a VBS or special service with a mindset of training the host and including the host will leave them more equipped to do things they never thought they could do.

Ending on Success!

I received a letter from a pastor in Mexico who wrote how thankful he was that we trained some of his youth. Before we came, none of the youth in his church felt comfortable helping teach in their Sunday school. After we worked with the youth and encouraged them to do one of the days of the short-term mission's Bible school, they were confident they could do it themselves, and their efforts continued after our group left, a wonderful ripple effect from our service.

Self-Preparation Exercise—Write out a prayer or meditation regarding why you are going on this trip and your expectations:

_____

_____

_____

_____

_____

_____

Getting Ready

We assume that you are a trip participant but not the organizer of the trip or leader of the group. If you are the trip organizer or a group leader, you should use our book, *Footsteps Short-Term Missions Leadership Handbook.* Your trip organizer will likely take care of most group arrangements, such as air fare, transportation in the host country, lodging, most meals, organizing supplies for your service project, arrangements with the host country ministry partner, and many more items.

Helping the Group Get Ready

As a team member you may want to offer to help with some of the logistics of getting the trip organized, and you may know others who cannot go on the trip but who would be willing to help. The timeline below gives you an idea of what the organizer likely has done or is now doing.

A Trip Organizer's Timeline for Preparing a Trip

Task	When	Calendar Dates, Subtasks, and Notes	☑
Costs Estimated	1 year in advance		
Market Trip	9 months to 1 year in advance		
Flights Scheduled	6 months in advance		
Logistics Arranged	4 to 6 months in advance		
Important Documents Prepped	2 to 4 months in advance		
Training Day or Days	1 to 2 months in advance		

This simplified checklist is the tip of the iceberg as to what your trip organizer has going on. There are many opportunities to help. Your efforts do need to be coordinated with the trip organizer, however, or you can make his or her job harder. The handy worksheet on the next page helps you identify areas where you might help your trip organizer.

The worksheet is based on abilities and tasks required for organizing a short-term mission. It can help you discuss with the trip organizer the ways you and those you know can help. Helpers do not necessarily need to be going on the trip. Look over the chart and discuss with your trip organizer.

"Who-Can-Help, How Can I Help?" Worksheet

Helper Name & Availability	Area	Skill or Attribute	Tasks They Can Do
	Research	- Internet access - Good phone skills	- Research mission options, partners - Scouting trip arrangements
	Written materials	- Writing, typing, layout or graphics skills	- Compose letters or edit your letters - Type, layout, and print specific handouts
	Recruiting	- Sales experience - Knows a lot of potential participants	- Recruiting strategy brainstorming - Develop materials - Give presentations
	Fundraising	- Knows a lot of potential donors - Raised funds for other charity	- Fundraising strategy brainstorming - Develop materials
	Airfare research	- Knows how to research airfares	- Scouting trip reservations - Mission trip reservations
	In-country travel, accommodations, and resources	- Research skills	- Travel – Hotels - Food - Fun activities - Support resources for the mission project, e.g., where to buy needed materials
	Ensure everyone has all documents filed or in hand	- Organizational skills	- Passports - Itineraries - Signed waivers
	Training	- Scheduling experience - Well organized - Experience in one of the following: teaching, mission trips, or the type of work in the service project	- Training logistics (place, time) - Write training day agenda - Arrange presenters and activity leaders - Confirm attendees - Give a presentation - Lead an activity

Your "To Do" List, Packing Lists, & List of Other Things to Remember

Apart from helping the group, you will need to make numerous small decisions about what you will bring. You will also have to do numerous small tasks that threaten to make your head spin and memory fail. A checklist of important documents can help you, for example, avoid leaving your passport on a copier 100 miles from the airport, as one mission trip participant discovered she had done. Unfortunately, she was at the airport when she realized this.

You will find it useful to have several types of packing lists and checklists. You may have heard of someone who is incredibly fit referred to as having "six-pack" abs. If you have the following "six-pack" of lists, you will be in great shape for your trip:

1. **"To Do" List**

2. **Personal Packing List**

3. **Luggage transfer checklist**—the luggage you need to get from point A to point B, for example, from plane to bus, and then from bus to hotel, and so on. This list helps you avoid getting two bags and a purse to the bus and then remembering you left a camera bag back in the baggage claim area. We provide a form on page 17.

4. **Items you're bringing and plan to leave there when you go home.** We provide a form on page 18.

5. **Items you are taking *and* bringing home** (a separate list from list #2)—It is often hard to remember what you will leave and what you will bring home. For example, you may be bringing books for the children's program that you will leave and sheet music you borrowed from your church that you must bring back. We provide a form on page 18.

6. **"Did You Remember...?" Checklist**—A list of things you don't want nagging you as you head to the airport... "Did I stop the newspapers?", "Did I turn the air conditioner off?", etc. We provide a base list on page 19.

"To Do" List

☑	Item
	Application (usually needs to be given to trip organizer)
	Liability and Covenant Release
	Deposit
	Get Passport, if needed
	Supply List for Donations (to share with friends or in the church for donations)
	Get Visas, if needed
	Immunizations
	Final Payment
	Trip Cancellation/Medical Insurance
	Copies of Passport (for luggage and for leader)
	Tentative Trip Schedule & Emergency Contacts
	Currency or Traveler's Checks
	Photocopy of Passport, Credit Cards, Health Insurance, & Drivers License in Each Bag
	Credit/ATM Cards and Contact #'s (in case lost)
	Health Documentation (especially of any allergies)
	List of Generic Names for Prescription Drugs
	Airplane/Transportation Tickets
	Emergency Information (contact person and phone #'s)
	Insurance (contact #'s and group/ individual policy #'s)
	Email Addresses (of people you want to send updates)

Add more items below.

☑	Item	☑	Item	☑	Item

- Make copies of your important documents and place a copy in each of your bags. This makes life much easier should you lose a credit card, or have a wallet, passport, or purse stolen. It is some work but well worth it in case of theft or loss.

- Frequent flier miles. Check if your airline has a frequent flier program or, better yet, if they partner with an airline you are likely to use in the future. Sign up before the trip and bring your number with you. Always ask staff to enter your number, even if they say you won't get miles—I have found many times that miles were still credited.

How to Create Your Personal Packing List

Your trip organizer may give you a suggested packing list for personal items. There are also many travel lists available on the Internet (on Google, for example, search for "travel packing list"). We provide a list below of common items that people take on mission trips. The lists that readers of this book will make will vary by their destinations, their age and lifestyle, time of year for the trip, the weather forecasts, and the service project. Since we can't give you the exact list, we will give you some hints that apply to many trips and let you customize a packing list for yourself.

We wouldn't expect you to bring everything on these lists—for one thing, you would be well over your weight limit. Instead, choose what fits your personal needs and add items not listed.

Clothing

Women
- ☐ Pajamas
- ☐ Undergarments
- ☐ Dresses (typically past knees)
- ☐ Blouses
- ☐ Pants and/or jeans
- ☐ Shorts (when appropriate)
- ☐ Swimwear (please be discreet)
- ☐ Socks and/or hosiery
- ☐ Shoes (dress and casual)
- ☐ Belt

- ☐ Sandals
- ☐ Jacket and/or sweater
- ☐ Work clothes

Men

- ☐ Pajamas
- ☐ Undergarments
- ☐ Dress pants
- ☐ Pants and/or jeans
- ☐ Shirts (include at least one dress shirt)
- ☐ Shorts (when appropriate)
- ☐ Swimwear (please be discreet)
- ☐ Socks
- ☐ Shoes (dress and casual)
- ☐ Belt
- ☐ Sandals
- ☐ Jacket and/or sweater
- ☐ Work clothes

Tip: use extreme caution so as not to offend our foreign hosts by bringing clothes that border on immodesty

Seasonal Items

Winter Items

- ☐ Gloves
- ☐ Hat or rain bonnet
- ☐ Boots
- ☐ Umbrella

Summer Items

- ☐ Sunglasses
- ☐ Suntan lotion
- ☐ Sunburn relief/aloe
- ☐ Hat or cap
- ☐ Toothbrush, toothpaste, & dental floss
- ☐ Skin care lotions/cream
- ☐ Bar soap and washcloth
- ☐ Cosmetics
- ☐ Compact mirror
- ☐ Perfume/cologne
- ☐ Deodorant
- ☐ Shampoo
- ☐ Hair brush/comb
- ☐ Shaving stuff
- ☐ Feminine hygiene
- ☐ Sewing kit

Tip: Dressing in layers will provide for a variety of temperature changes.

Personal Items
- ☐ Laundry bag or garbage bag
- ☐ Zip-close plastic bags
- ☐ Camera & film
- ☐ Video camera, tapes, battery, & charger
- ☐ Towel
- ☐ Journal
- ☐ Flashlight
- ☐ Bible
- ☐ Phrase book or electronic translator
- ☐ Alarm clock
- ☐ Reading materials
- ☐ Snacks (favorite compact ones)
- ☐ Pre-addressed mailing labels
- ☐ Eye shades
- ☐ Ear plugs
- ☐ Neck pillow
- ☐ Fanny pack with water bottle
- ☐ Small tissue packets
- ☐ Moist towelettes
- ☐ Hair dryer
- ☐ Converters and adapters
- ☐ Pocket knife
- ☐ Money pouch
- ☐ Detergent
- ☐ Laundry line & hangers

Hints for Packing Clothes

- Carry at least one change of clothes and toiletries in your carry-on bag. If your bag is lost, you will have two pairs of clothes that you can use until you can get others.

- Pack clothes that can be used in layers. If it gets too hot you can take a layer off. If it gets too cold (common on an airplane) then you can add a sweatshirt.

- Check what the weather usually is during the trip's time to make clothing choices, and then check the actual weather a few days before you go. Websites such as weather.com may have conditions in your host country (an Internet search for "weather websites" will give you many options). Your local partners can give you additional information as to what the weather info really means (lots of mud, cold at night, etc.).

- Bring trash bags and zip-close plastic bags for dirty/wet clothes

- Bring clothes that you can give away. You may find that the people are so poor that the clothes you are wearing would make welcome gifts. Find out from your host country partners if this would be appropriate and not offensive, and when you leave you can literally leave the clothes off your back (well, except for the ones you need for the flight home). An indirect gift, such as giving a package of clothes to the church for a rummage sale, rather than giving individual items to people may be a prudent approach. While you might arrange to bring clothes that you can give away, they should be in reasonable condition, the equivalent of what would be suitable for sale at a U.S. thrift store.

Other Considerations

- Pack insect repellent, if appropriate for the destination. The best prevention for many diseases is not getting bitten by the bugs that carry them. If your destination has mosquitoes, you may want something with DEET (it has some toxicity so read the directions carefully).

- Bring sunscreen and use it. You may be outside more than you are used to and in an unfamiliar climate, where you can't gauge your sun exposure very well.

- Typically each person is allowed two bags of up to 50 pounds each on international flights—

Tip: For mosquitoes, sand fleas (often called no-see-ums) and minor bug problems, consider something like Cactus Juice. Created on the island of Roatan, Honduras, it is a natural bug repellent and SPF 20 sunscreen. It is made out of cactus and actually smells good (like citrus).

Some people have also had success with taking B-complex vitamins for a few weeks before a trip and report that bugs bother them less.

the same limit as on most domestic flights. The international limit until recently had commonly been two 70-pound bags. Some carriers may still allow this higher limit. If you have domestic flights as part of the trip or intercontinental flights or are using a low-cost carrier, the limits may be lower (e.g., Air Asia). If your trip organizer hasn't done so, check with your airline for its current restrictions on dimensions and weight.

- Offer to designate one piece of your luggage for service items.

Luggage Transfer Checklist

Describe each piece of your luggage next to each box and check the boxes when making sure all items are present. This will make it much easier to keep track of everything during the chaos of transitions. When your group is transferring, from a plane or other vehicle, use this checklist to make sure everything is there.

❑

❑

❑

❑

Tip: Use a digital camera to take pictures of your luggage and print out a couple copies. This can ensure you will describe the piece accurately if it is lost, and you can easily tell someone which bag to look for if you've asked someone to pick up a piece of your luggage.

Tip: Make multiple copies of this page to use whenever you need to confirm your luggage is with you. Having multiple copies may also allow you to have someone else do a count or pick up your luggage for you.

Items You're Bringing to Leave in Country

❑

❑

❑

❑

❑

Items that Return Home

❑

❑

❑

❑

❑

"Did You Remember... ?" Checklist

The time right before you leave is usually a flurry of activity. One person we know left in such a hurry that he left his front door wide open—for three weeks. (The screen door was closed.) Amazingly, nothing was out of order in his house when he returned. The following list gives you a base that will help you make your own list of what to remember:

House Details

- ☐ Stop newspaper
- ☐ Notify neighbors of absence
- ☐ Turn off unnecessary appliances (e.g. water heater)
- ☐ Turn down furnace/air conditioning
- ☐ Pay bills that will come due during absence
- ☐ Back up important computer files and store at place other than your house
- ☐ Stop postal service
- ☐ Leave house key and itinerary with friends or family
- ☐ Provide care for pets, landscaping, and plants
- ☐ Clean refrigerator of perishables
- ☐ Secure home
- ☐ Set up timed lighting
- ☐ Turn down thermostat
- ☐ Eliminate fire hazards
- ☐ Arrange rides to and from airport
- ☐ Close and lock front door. ☺

Add your "Did You Remember... ?" items below.

✓	Item	✓	Item	✓	Item

Prepping Your Medical Kit & Other Travel Medicine Topics

We have found that some common sense guidelines can help you in the medical situations encountered on a service trip. I am not a physician and this guide is not a substitute for a first-aid guide or for the services of a medical professional in the field. If you feel sick, call a physician.

Get emergency medical insurance. You may say "oh, my insurance covers me in case of an emergency while I am away." Most insurance companies do not cover medical evacuation if you need to be airlifted from outside the United States. The bill may be $15,000 to $25,000 or more. It is worth the few extra dollars to insure against this. Footsteps offers a variety of insurance possibilities, as do other carriers.

Get your immunizations early. Many really "cruddy" diseases out there can be easily prevented by taking some medication during your trip or getting a simple shot. The U.S. government's Centers for Disease Control (CDC) lists recommendations by country and region. Go to www.footstepsmissions.org for links to this valuable information. Encourage each person to go to his or her doctor or community travel clinic well before departure.

Your group should bring a good-quality medical kit—and have someone look through it before you leave. There is nothing more frustrating than looking through a medical kit for anti-diarrhea medicine only to find out that your kit, although large in size, is made up of little else than 4,000 band aids. Here are some suggestions that Steve Bander, M.D., a friend of Footsteps, has suggested as helpful additions to any medical kit (all of these items can be purchased over the counter, generic versions are fine; the following are the most common brand medications with the generic name in brackets):

- Benadryl [diphenhydramine hydrochloride] or Claritin [loratadine] (for allergic reactions)
- Benadryl cream (for itching and irritation)
- Advil or Aleve [ibuprofen] (pain, fever, & anti-inflammatory)

- Tylenol [acetaminophen] (pain and fever)
- Zantac [ranitidine] (for acid or indigestion)
- Pepto-Bismol [bismuth subsalicylate] (for diarrhea, and it acts as an antibiotic for certain stomach viruses, for prevention take one tablet before each meal)
- Hydrocortisone (for itching/rashes; do not put on face!)
- Aloe Vera Jelly
- Lamisil [terbinafine hydrochloride] (for fungal infection)
- Neosporin [polymyxin B sulfate, bacitracin zinc, neomycin] (for infections, skin abrasions or cuts)
- Immodium AD [loperamide] (controls acute diarrhea)
- Sam Splints (for sprains, fractures or bone stabilization—use with an ace wrap)
- Ace Wraps (for wrapping wounds and for sprains)

Provide your trip leader any critical medical history, especially information on allergies. It can make a life or death difference if someone caring for you knows this at the right time.

Make sure your trip leader has a list of any serious medications you are taking in case you are incapacitated and a medical care person needs to know what you are taking. Ask your physicians for the generic names of the medications you are taking in case you need to identify the medication to a non-English speaking pharmacist who may not know the brand name. Keep the list separate from your medications.

Have your trip organizer locate the closest medical care facilities. Before you go or right away upon your arrival, your trip leader should find out where the closest medical facility is located, what they can and can't provide, and have a plan of action on how to contact the facility and how to get people to it as fast as possible. Having a plan and the information can save critical time in an emergency. This information may be difficult to find out if you have limited language abilities and are in a crisis situation. There is a place in the "Important Info" pages for this information. It is also a good idea that more than one person has this information—it may be your trip leader who needs help.

Bring any important medical devices or medications in your carry-on bags. Unfortunately luggage is often lost in transit. If you have a large medical device, let the airline staff know that it is important for you to keep it with you. They can be very accommodating in situations like this.

Visit the dentist. If you haven't been to the dentist lately or you know you have a dental problem that needs to be taken care of, you should do so well before the trip. You do not want to be out in the field and suddenly have that old toothache flare up or have your wisdom teeth need pulling.

CPR and Choking First Aid. Consider a class or a refresher.

AVOID GETTING SICK!

Before each meal or snack wash your hands or use hand sanitizer. Do this in a way that doesn't offend your host country partners. It doesn't make sense that using a sanitizer lotion is an offense toward the food preparation or the preparer's cleanliness but it has been taken that way. Be discreet—for example, don't make a big display of using sanitizer at the table.

Recommended Medical Books

Here are some high-quality books and resources you may want to consider. If you have a physician in your group, he or she might appreciate having one of these titles. Most are small enough to take with you as a valuable resource.

Comprehensive Guide to Wilderness and Travel Medicine by Eric Weiss. Small enough to carry but packed with info, including how to take care of things without the normal equipment.

Field Guide to Wilderness Medicine by Paul Auerbach, Howard Donner, and Eric Weiss. This field guide focuses on information needed when medical situations present in wilderness settings. Good for the physician in your group.

The Travel and Tropical Medicine Handbook by Elaine Jong. This respected manual offers the latest advice on preventing, evaluating, and managing diseases that can be acquired in tropical environments and foreign countries.

The Traveler's Natural Medicine Kit by Pamela Hirsch. Easy and effective remedies for staying healthy on the road.

Wilderness Medical Associates Field Guide by Jim Morrissey. The huge list of topics cover major medical emergencies you may encounter away from medical help.

Sharing the Trip: Involving Your Church & Community

A short-term mission is a unique adventure. There are likely many in your church and community who would like to live this experience but can't because of their situations in life, work, or family. A mission trip can do good things for the host country and have a "ripple effect" of creating energy and motivation for people at home. By making use of the following suggestions, you can help those at home to be a part of your trip in spirit, even though they can't go physically.

Prayer Reminders. Make some creative reminders to help people pray for you while you are on your trip. This might be a picture of your team or a calendar with your team's picture for the month you are gone.

Email updates during the trip, with photos when possible, to partners and friends. Don't count on email access, however. Many places with access have slow email. If you use online email, such as MSN, Hotmail or Yahoo!, create a list before you go that's saved on your online account so that you don't have to type any email addresses in and you are sending one email to the entire group. Large photo files sometimes do not send easily. It's often best to send pictures that are less than a megabyte, which may require taking lower resolution pictures or opening a picture file and saving a low-res copy on the computer you are using. Then you still have your high-res photo files when you get home.

Call during a service and talk live to the congregation. This may require a little work technically at home to connect your call to the audio system but can be a great way to share firsthand what is going on in your place of service and an effective way to transmit excitement about the mission to those at home. Be sure to take time zone differences into account.

Send a postcard. Get some postcards and send them to your partners at home. Write down a brief note about your service or something exciting or new you experienced and mail it from that country. Don't forget to take the addresses of those you want to send to (you can use the address section of this book).

Helping Your Group Find Resources

Financial Support. Financial contributors can serve vicariously through you. Before the trip, write letters to people who might support you or the mission. A letter writing party can get things started. The "Partner Communication Center" on page 127 has forms to keep track of donor addresses.

Donated & Loaned Items. Coordinate asking for equipment and supply donations with your trip organizer. Use the sample on page 25 to create a flyer that fits your specific needs. Place a picture of one of the projects, crafts, or even of the country you are visiting on it so people can see a little bit more about your trip. When listing the items, you may want to provide an approximate dollar amount so that people can donate the money to purchase the item if they don't already have it to loan or donate.

Wanted: Donations of Supplies and Equipment to Help our Trip to [Insert Host Country Name]

On [insert date of trip] a team of volunteers will be going to [insert host country] to help in a variety of ways. You may be able to help us get supplies or borrow equipment, so we can provide the best service and maximize our impact.

If you have any of the items on the list below that we can use, please either:

- drop them off in the box marked "Mission Group" at the back of the church, or

- check off the items that you are interested in donating or loaning and provide your contact information so we can arrange a convenient time to get them from you.

Let us know how much of a specific item you can donate.

If you don't have any of the items and still want to help, you can donate money to purchase a specific item for the trip.

Thanks for your help. It's great to be a part of a caring community interested in making a difference around the world.

- Item 1
- Item 2
- Item 3, and so on.

Name:
Address:

Phone:
E-mail:

[you might include this message]

Please place this in the offering plate or send to the following address: [add your address here]

Important Information "All in One Place"

Use this worksheet to compile info "all in one place" for easy reference. (Note: airline contact info and airport codes can be found in the Appendices.)

Flight Information

Contact Person   Contact Info

Travel Agency

Airline 1

Airline 2

Airline 3

Airline 4

Flight Schedule... Don't forget to confirm 48–72 hours before flight!

Dates	Airline & Flight #	Record Locators	Depart Time & City	Arrival Time & City

Emergency Contacts & Numbers

In the U.S.

Out of U.S.

Emergency & Medical Evacuation Insurance Provider

Group Number

Contact Number/s

Contact Person (if any)

Your Plan if Someone is Hurt in Country

What are the medical facilities closest to the places the group will be spending time? (name, contact information, what type of services or care available)

How far away are these facilities and how would you transport a hurt group member to them.

Embassy Information

(Can be found on www.footstepsmissions.org)

Countries Visiting	Ambassador	Embassy Numbers	Office Hours

Service Partner Info

Dates	Organization/Person	Contact #'s	Schedule Notes

Transportation Information

U.S. Transportation Name or Organization   Contact Info

(Note that contact information for many rental companies and driving information can be found in the Appendices.)

Destination Country Transport Info

Dates	Organization/Person	Contact #'s	Schedule Notes

Notes:

Accommodations Info

U.S. Pre- or Post-trip Hotel/Homestay   Contact Info

Destination Country Accommodations Info

Dates	Organization/Person	Contact #'s	Schedule Notes

Notes:

How Much Will it Cost?

One of the first questions you will have for the person organizing the trip is, "What will it cost?" Generally, the organizer will give you an estimate of what the trip will cost. An estimate is just that—an estimate. It may change. Usually, final costs are reliably set two months before the trip.

Different organizers will include different items in the cost of what you pay to them. For example, some include all meals, while others cover only some meals, expecting that you will sometimes eat out on your own. Other out-of-pocket costs may include snacks, excursions, optional activities, water, extra drinks at meals, and, of course, souvenirs.

What your group fee pays for

If the trip organizer doesn't give you a good list of what you are paying for with your trip fee, you should ask. The first page of the following budget worksheet gives you a list of the major expenses that are usually, but not always, covered in the fee you pay to the trip organizer. You can use it to identify all that is included in your particular group fee. If the item is something that you will pay, you can check the appropriate box and write in the amount you expect to pay out of pocket.

What you might pay for out of pocket

Page two of the budget worksheet lists items for which you usually pay some or all of the cost out of pocket. Of course, most trips include much of the food cost in the main fee, but snacks and some meals will likely be in addition. You will have a lot of discretion for most of the items on page two. Will you plan to give gifts to your host country partners? Will you bring gifts home for friends, family, or supporters? You might want to research what kinds of souvenirs are available to get an idea if there are appropriate gifts for the people you are considering as recipients. The "Money Questions" section (page 34) provides a list of questions that can help you fill out your budget worksheet and answer the question, **"How much money should I bring?"**

Budget Worksheet	Paid by Group	Paid by You	Estimated Out-of-Pocket Costs (not in group trip fee)
Trip Promotion			
T-shirts / Team Apparel			
Training Costs for Team			
Visas			
Immunizations			
Scholarship Funds			
Transportation			
Flights			
Airport Fees / Departure Tax			
Vehicle Rental (in country)			
Vehicle Insurance			
Driver (in country)			
Fuel			
Other Transportation			
Guides			
Lodging + Taxes			
Transaction Fees			
Service Supplies			
Gift Given by Group (your contribution toward)			
Excursions with Group			
Medical Travel Insurance			
Other			
Other			
Totals			

Budget Worksheet	Paid by Group	Paid by You	Estimated Out-of-Pocket Costs (not in group trip fee)
Food +Tips & Taxes			
Breakfast			
Snacks			
Bottled Water / Soda			
Lunch			
Dinner			
Other Drinks			
Trip Cancellation Insurance			
Taxis, Bus, Car Cost During Free Time			
Entertainment Options, not part of group fee			
Tips for Personal Services			
Computer Access Charges			
Misc. Incidentals (batteries, sunblock, etc.)			
Toiletries/Medicines			
Mailing Packages Home			
Phone Card or Calls			
Postcards			
Stamps			
Souvenirs for Self			
Gift for:			
Gift for:			
Gift for:			
Gift for:			
Totals			

Money Questions to Research

Your trip leader may have researched some of the following questions. Your other group members may be doing their own research, too, so pool information. There are many Internet forums about travel to specific parts of the world. You can sometimes find someone who has been to your destination country who is a good source of information. As with all Internet information, don't take it as Gospel.

Will I need spending money?

What kinds of souvenirs, crafts, or gifts are available and what are the price ranges?

Are there items commonly offered that are illegal or unethical to buy?

When will be the best opportunities during our trip to buy souvenirs?

Is bargaining expected? Is it culturally wrong or hurtful not to bargain?

Are U.S. dollars accepted in most places and is the exchange rate usually O.K. or part of bargaining?

Best places to exchange money in this country:

Worst places to exchange money in this country:

Is it a good idea to bring local currency (exchange $ in U.S. before the trip)?

Will there be opportunities, including time, to exchange money...

Upon arriving at the airport (check hours exchange is open):

At the following hotels you will be staying at or near:

At banks in the following places:

Typical bank hours in this country:

At post offices in the following places:

Are there laws against exchanging money at nonofficial locations and do you need to keep records of money exchanged in country?

Are traveler's checks commonly accepted in the area you will be visiting? Is the traveler's check exchange rate different from the cash exchange rate?

Your credit card's exchange rate:

Note that there is a trend for credit cards to charge a fee for a transaction in a foreign country.

Other $ advice:

Read the fine print, not just the big signs, at money exchanges. Some exchanges prominently post the "sell rate" for U.S. dollars, not the "buy rate," so you may think you are getting a better rate if you don't look closely. Some exchanges may list a rate for very large amounts of dollars and have a much worse rate for smaller amounts.

Beware ATMs. They may charge high fees that are in addition to what your credit card company or bank charge. Use at your own risk!

A reality check: What is the typical hourly or daily wage in the area you are visiting?

Scheduling for Short-Term Missions

A schedule can help you feel purposeful and on task. Don't become ruled by what you write down, however. One of the primary keys to a successful trip is to be flexible and adaptable. In the United States, we tend to be ruled by the clock. This is often not the case in host countries.

Most of the time, your trip leader will be setting the daily schedule and it will depend on many arrangements and conditions that you might not be aware of. The ideal schedule that follows the tips that we list here may not be possible on your trip. The host partner may need things to happen a certain way or your choice of service project demands a different schedule.

Ask your trip leader for a time to discuss scheduling issues if you see a need and work to consolidate your questions so they can be taken care of in one session. Imagine if twenty people in your group had just one question each when a daily schedule is handed out. Your group would get nothing done for the first hour of the day. Part of being a mission team is working within the schedule for the entire group.

Seven Keys to Highly Effective Scheduling

1. **When scheduling your service each day, it's ideal to have either the morning, afternoon, or evening off**. Even though you are coming to serve, you also need time to synthesize all that you are learning and to interact with the culture and people.

2. **Each week, schedule at least one day off for relaxation.** It may mean going to church on Sunday and then doing laundry and just hanging out. If you have lots of energy, you can go sightseeing. This is especially important on trips that are three weeks or longer.

Tip: On a long trip that lasts more than four weeks, many people hit a "homesick wall" four weeks to eight weeks after leaving home. It is natural and may be helped by scheduling some extra free time to relax and work with one's feelings.

3. **Schedule time to see some of the culture, country, and people.** Although the service is the foundation of the trip, this is an important part of the learning experience—don't discount its importance. Take advantage of opportunities for some fun, one day a week or more, to see some of the sights, eat out, and learn from the people.

4. **Schedule time to become accustomed to your new environment.** Fear of the unknown weighs heavily on many who go far from home to serve. Your group may do an activity like the scavenger hunt on page 58. If your group doesn't do this, you might find a buddy in the group and set some similar tasks to do together that get you using local transportation, learning the lay of the land, and interacting with the people.

5. **Use your "Energy Barometer" to adjust your schedule.** Watch for signs of exhaustion, such as impatience with personality differences and sharpened annoyance at pet peeves. Go to bed earlier, even if you have to leave off doing something interesting. Pray for each other regarding energy levels.

6. **Schedule time for the unexpected**. If your schedule is too tight, you risk catastrophe when something unexpected happens (and it will happen). Leave some breathing room between events.

7. **Schedule for a herd of snails not gazelles.** Groups do not move quickly. Expect it will take time to get the group together, with bathroom stops, eating, etc. With a group of 15 or more, any stop is going to take at least 30 minutes, even a "quick" bathroom run before the bus leaves.

This may require patience on your part as you continually wait for the slowest team member to finish. Expect this time will be there, part of the trip. Use it to observe where you are, even if it's a simple bus stop. Use it to talk with your group members or locals. Use it to take a deep breath and be with your thoughts for a moment. Consider the time a gift of a "Patience Builder." If you shift from considering this time "wasted" to seeing it as an opportunity to enrich your experience, you will build your capacity for patience. You may even begin welcoming these inevitable delays. Each Patience Builder below can be repeated as many times as you need to.

Seven Types of Patience Builders

1. Observe something around you that you would not see in the United States. Describe it or draw it on some paper. What else can you say about it?

2. Listen and identify a sound you wouldn't hear in the United States. Describe it. What else can you say about it.

3. Identify a smell that you wouldn't encounter in the United States. Describe it. What else can you say about it?

4. Ask a group member a conversational question, such as the following: What got them interested in the trip? What did they think of breakfast/lunch/dinner/the recent weather/any recent trip event?

5. Ask a group member a philosophical question? What do you think about the complexities of helping the poor? Why is it sometimes thought of as wrong-minded? Attitudes towards the poor in the U.S. often differ from attitudes towards the poor in other countries, why do you think that is?

6. Say a few words to a local who is not part of your ministry partner group. If appropriate, try to use the local language to ask a question. It can be as simple as saying your name and asking his or her name.

7. Collect your thoughts. What is coming up today that matters to me? How can I make it matter in the way I want it to? Alternatively, consider the day just past or some event that has already happened.

The following pages contain forms where you can write down your schedule information.

Weekly Schedule Forms

Week One	Mon	Tue	Wed	Thur	Fri	Sat	Sun
morning							
afternoon							
evening							

Other Scheduling Notes

Week Two

	Mon	Tue	Wed	Thur	Fri	Sat	Sun
morning							
afternoon							
evening							

Other Scheduling Notes

Week Three

	Mon	Tue	Wed	Thur	Fri	Sat	Sun
morning							
afternoon							
evening							

Other Scheduling Notes

Week Four

	Mon	Tue	Wed	Thur	Fri	Sat	Sun
morning							
afternoon							
evening							

Other Scheduling Notes

Week Five

	Mon	Tue	Wed	Thur	Fri	Sat	Sun
morning							
afternoon							
evening							

Other Scheduling Notes

Week Six

	Mon	Tue	Wed	Thur	Fri	Sat	Sun
morning							
afternoon							
evening							

Other Scheduling Notes

Being a Good Servant on the Team

As short-term mission team member, you have a unique, needed and adventurous opportunity before you. You're the backbone of the trip. You're a co-laborer in expanding the Kingdom. You get to help other believers in other places of the world in different ways than you ever have before. Understanding your role and the roles of your co-laborers has the potential of making a trip great or horrible—vote for great. Here are some things that can help.

- **Strive to be servant of all.** In Mark 9:33–37 Jesus settled an argument among the disciples as to who was greatest. "Do you want to be first?" he asked, "Then you have to be last." You have to be the servant of all. This is a powerful stance of humility... seeing what needs to be done and doing it, noticing that your teammate is discouraged and encouraging him or her, and doing more than you thought you would to help your team accomplish His goals.

- **Know the difference between your needs and wants.** Do you have to have the bus stop because you suddenly got hungry? Do you have to call home NOW? (In some settings, you may not be able to communicate with home short of an emergency). You're a vegetarian in a meat-eating country. Hmmm? Does the group have to search high and low for vegetarian cuisine, or did you bring enough energy bars to get you through a long run of meaty meals?

- **You are not there to personally save everyone in the host country.** We are all called to witness but not all called to evangelism. Sometimes your host needs you to do things that sow seeds, so they can share Jesus effectively later. Sowing can come in many forms: cleaning the church or stadium for an event, painting walls, taking care of children, distributing groceries, and so on.

- **Let go of American ideas of closure.** Let's consider an example. We go to build a house. The materials are late and the promised cement mixer is broken. It becomes obvious you will not get the glory of finishing the project before your plane leaves. Frustrations grow and intense work ensues... until a sense of failure emerges.

Let go of that feeling. Leaving something unfinished can be a failure if the locals have no means to continue with the work—think that through before you choose a project—BUT it can often give your partners more ownership in the project and decrease dependencies on outsiders to "do it all." The unfinished house may give them opportunities to step out in faith, unify and take on the task themselves. Your incomplete task may be part of how God wants the project to unfold.

- **Let go of American attitudes of superiority**. Americans have a lot to give: English language skills, organizational skills, technology, what can look like fantastic wealth and educational opportunities, and on and on. It can be intimidating to host-country partners and become a barrier to an effective relationship. If the American takes on the mind-set of *coming alongside* the host partners rather than *coming as an authority*, a long-lasting relationship has a much greater chance of resulting. Instead of entering the host country with "all the answers," it is a richer experience to come with questions... to be a listener and a learner.

- **Understand what your leader's role is *NOT***

  - Your leader is *NOT* there to make sure you have everything you want, or even to make you comfortable, or to make your personal agenda happen. As a servant, you are susceptible to a subtle thought sneaking in: "someone should be serving me..." and that someone should be the leader.

  - Your leader is not Superman. Your leader will get tired, hungry and frustrated like you. Your leader can't run without getting tired, will not have instant solutions to every problem, and can't do it all. Your leader cannot function alone. He or she will need you and your teammates to encourage and make things happen.

- Your leader is *NOT* always there for you. Your leader may need to step away from a project to set up for the next day or to troubleshoot a problem. If your leader is not with you, it does not mean he or she is escaping work to sit on the beach.

- Your leader is *NOT* all-knowing. He or she is not a tour guide who knows what kind of rock formation that is, or where you can get the best deal on local baskets, or if the chicken was cooked in olive oil (or if it's really chicken), what the weather is at home, why your cell phone doesn't work, and so on.

- **So what IS the role of your leader?**

  - Your leader is a facilitator. Your leader is there to lay the groundwork so your group and the host people have chance at a successful ministry.

  - Your leader is there to guide the group and keep you on task.

  - Your leader is there to keep you focused on Jesus.

  - Your leader is there to help you to fly… to learn and grow in new ways.

  - Your leader is the team captain. He or she may need to make decisions that are good for the group but not popular with you as an individual.

Using a Translator

Address the audience. A natural tendency is to talk to the translator. Think of your translator as if he or she were a sound system speaker. You don't talk *to* the loudspeaker, it just projects your words. The same is true of your translator.

Use short sections/sentences. Don't talk too long without letting the translator speak. If you say too much, the translator will inevitably paraphrase and lose some meaning. For an important sentence, pause before saying it so that the translator says everything up it; then say the sentence, stop and look to the translator. The sentence will have a larger dramatic effect.

Be careful about using big words, technical terms. One friend of ours spent several minutes explaining the word paradigm to the translator and lost the audience.

Be careful using idioms, sayings, metaphors, or slang. "He hit a home run" is meaningless in Russia, where baseball is almost unknown but soccer is a dominant sport. Depending on the translator, a phrase using a metaphor such as, "We'll tackle that project tomorrow," can be bewildering.

Let the translator finish.

Look to each other for cues to continue.

Be careful about using places or names that may be unfamiliar to them. For example, "Colin Powell did a great job trying to facilitate peace" or "We were in Yosemite and almost fell off a cliff." Instead say, "The United States head diplomat, Secretary of State Colin Powell, did a great job" and "We were in one of the large parklands in the United States, called Yosemite. It has mountains and steep trails and we almost fell off a cliff." These give the local translator the information he or she needs to choose a description that fits the audience's background. If the audience understands who Colin Powell is or what Yosemite is, the translator will likely leave out the rest. If the other information is needed, you've given it.

Service Preparation

There are so many different types of service that we can't cover preparation for specific projects in this book. We can give you some principles that apply to all service. First, service training should prepare the group to change the service, if needed. Oddly, you should prepare to be ready to do something you didn't exactly prepare to do. You may learn more once you are in your host country, and your actual service may end up being something very different. God does not always tell us what His plan is in a way we can plan for. Earlier in this book, we discussed the importance of choosing a service project that is a "real need" of the host ministry partner. An important part of preparing for service is understanding how the service choice meets a real need—at least what we think is the real need before you get there.

Second, service training should prepare the group to do its planned project, especially how to be a disciplined work group. Despite the group needing to be open to changes, the group's training should end with it ready in some detail to do its project. Note that host ministries list poor preparation as one of the top three reasons missions fail. The following three categories should by covered for the specific project:

- **Supplies**: Identify what you will need to bring, how you will get the supplies, and how you will get them to the ministry site.

- **Skills:** Identify what skills are needed, who will perform actions needing them, and who needs a refresher or lessons on certain skills.

- **Project Management:** Who will direct different parts of the project? Who is the overall leader? What role will locals play in this? If you don't know the locals yet, do you have a time set aside to identify their skills and bring them onto the team or task groups? Is there a plan to get locals ready to continue or finish the project when the short-term group leaves? What is the project calendar? Do some things need to happen before others can? For example, cement may need to set before building a frame. Identify those things and who will monitor and give the go ahead to continue the project.

Third, service training needs to affirm the servant attitude. Consider Proverbs 3:9:

Honor the Lord with your wealth, with the first fruits of all your crops; then your barns will be filled to overflowing, and your vats will brim over with new wine.

This verse helps avoid an attitude problem that short-term mission participants, unfortunately, often fall into. Many have the perception that because they are going to serve where the people have little they don't need to give their best service, or their best in supplies, or even their best in preparation. The host country people perceive this—and appropriately so—as disrespectful. They also, and most often incorrectly, see the person with this attitude as insincere and that the message this person is delivering is insincere. On the other hand, if we strive to give our "first fruits," we honor God with our service and avoid these problems. Practically, team service preparation can strive for a "first fruits" attitude by acting on the following recommendations and examples.

Detailed Recommendations & Examples

Set realistic dates for getting your piece of the service project ready. This also includes getting the supplies. See page 23–25 for more on how to involve others for help getting these resources.

Practice any music, productions, stories, or testimonies that might be done in front of audiences. Practice makes confident.

Consult experts to teach or improve skills specific to your project. If you have a project that requires specific skills that can be learned in a session or two, consider asking people with good teaching skills and knowledge of that skill to work with you or your group. These teachers do not have to be going on the trip. Even if you have skilled people going on the trip, not having them do all the teaching of others can be good in not overloading them and getting some additional energy into the preparation. Plus, your skilled people have an opportunity to get another expert's input into the group's plan of attack for the project.

Pack Smart. Pack your supplies so they are easily accessible. Pack tools together for a specific project. For example, if you are cutting lumber in one project and building a bathroom in another, pack saws for the first project together and the tools for building the bathroom together. For the daily vacation Bible school, pack the supplies you need for each day together and label them. That way you don't have to take everything with you every day or open all your boxes and bags each day you are there.

Suggest a Packing Party for Service Supplies. It can be overwhelming if responsibility for all supplies rests on one person (imagine packing 20 suitcases by yourself—I have seen this happen). Instead, just before the trip, the team and others who might be interested in helping can get together to pack. The trip leader can divvy up responsibility for the bags among several team members.

Don't bring your trash as donations. I have seen this often where someone donates a broken computer and says, "All it needs is some fixing and it will work great." It is likely the people to whom it is going don't have the skills or the resources to fix it. If you have a computer that needs fixing, fix it and then donate it.

Bring some extra money to give out as gifts for those who help you, for unexpected projects, or even in case your well-planned program needs to be adjusted.

Conflict Resolution

Conflicts are inevitable on a short-term trip. This section was developed with the help of Darrah Garvin, Ph.D., staff psychologist, Peninsula Covenant Church, Redwood City, California. It offers a step by step way for you to resolve conflict.

Try the following steps, in order.

Pray. Ask the Lord to give you a servant's heart.

Initiate a talk appropriately. Use good timing and give everyone as much privacy as possible. A conflict might escalate if you confront the parties in public.

Start with an empathic statement. Try to relate to the person as much as possible.

Establish mutual trust and acceptance. Without some trust and acceptance of one another, the conflict is unlikely to be managed.

Determine the core of the conflict. We often mislead ourselves and manage the symptoms instead of discovering the central issue or core. If you move away from the perspective of the core, your chances of managing the conflict are lessened.

Analyze your assumptions and values. Once you determine the core of the conflict, you can, with the other party, look at the underlying assumptions. What does the other party assume about the conflict? What do you assume? Solutions will probably focus on the assumptions in common. At this stage, an analysis of values of each party can help.

Brainstorm creative alternatives to manage the conflict and turn the situation into a "positive."

Evaluate the alternatives according to rewards versus risks and select an option that makes use of the strengths of the parties.

Commit and covenant. Once you have chosen a method, commit or covenant to use that method. You may covenant with one another or yourself.

Evaluate. Finally, assess the outcome. Did the alternative chosen manage the conflict?

Alternative Methods of Resolving Conflict on Short-Term Missions

- Dueling pistols
  (note: don't bring in carry-on bags)
- Rock, paper, scissors
- Draw straws, decide whose drawing looks more like a real straw
- You divide, I choose
  (Solomon solution, better for cake than babies)
- Youngest first
- Biggest wins
- Flip a coin and switch argument to be over which side of local coin is tails and which is heads
- Play dead (opossums only)
- Thumb fight!
- Offer chocolate
- Must argue in Armenian
- Fake insanity... or don't fake...
- Redirect—Look, there's a squirrel

Learning Your Host Country's Culture

You want to be a good servant and respectful friend to those you meet. That requires you to be a student of the culture you are visiting. The following questions can take you quite a ways toward better cultural understanding. The first set regards your current thoughts. For the second set, "Basic Facts," the Internet can be a good resource, as well as the travel section of your bookstore. The advanced questions might require finding someone from that culture and having a long, frank conversation over coffee or dinner.

Preconceptions Exercise

Jot down notes, so you can compare this with what you learn in your research and what you learn through the experience of your trip. Use separate paper for longer answers.

1. What are the first thoughts or images that you think of regarding the country you are visiting?

2. What is your current understanding of where you are going?

3. How do you think the people's lives will be different from yours?

4. How will they be the same?

5. How do you think their spirituality is different from yours? You might consider behavior, beliefs, ritual, expression, attitudes.

6. How do you think their spiritual situation is the same as yours?

Basic Facts Collection

7. What countries or bodies of water surround the country you are visiting?

8. Name the capital and other major cities.

9. What are the primary religions?

10. What is the population?

11. What are some common foods specific to the country?

12. Who is the head of the country and what is his/her title?

13. What type of government does the country have?

14. What languages are spoken in the country?

15. What currency do they use and what is the exchange rate?

16. What is the income per capita?

17. What are the primary industries for the country?

18. Find a historical fact or event regarding the country?

19. Write out (phonetically) how locals say these words:
    - Hello   _____
    - Thanks   _____
    - I'm sorry   _____

Advanced Culture & History Activity

20. What are some behaviors that are considered particularly impolite in this culture (especially those that are different from typical U.S. attitudes)?

21. What are the culture's traditions and meanings associated with gift-giving?

22. How do the roles of men and women differ in this culture?

23. What would be inappropriate attire that a group member might wear?

24. What is the history of outside missionaries and workers in this country and in this particular community?

25. What is the history of the U.S. government's relations with this country? What do the locals think of United States citizens?

Scavenger Hunt Sample

When you arrive at your host country, a scavenger hunt has proven to be a fun and effective way to introduce a mission group to a country. The game helps people challenge themselves to get acclimated to unfamiliar surroundings. Through the exercise, you can encourage them to use local transportation, try some unique foods, and learn a little about the culture. The activity can help people later in the trip make good use of their free time. The best time to do this is at the beginning of the trip. Form small group "teams" and allocate a couple of hours. Here is a sample scavenger hunt that you can use to base yours on.

Sample: Costa Rica Fact Finding Mission

For each question or challenge you need to perform a task or find an answer from a Costa Rican. You will need to have this signed by a "Tico" confirming that you completed the tasks. For the questions you need to write in the answer.

1. Find and eat or drink guanabana
2. How big is the military in Costa Rica?
3. Who is Costa Rica's president?
4. How much of Costa Rica's Land is National Park?
5. Find the name of two major volcanoes in Costa Rica.
6. Find and eat jocotes
7. Find the names of two major parks in Costa Rica.
8. The egg from what sea animal is considered an aphrodisiac?
9. Find a tapir and draw a picture of it here:
10. What does waving your index finger from side to side mean?
11. When using Spanish in Costa Rica, how do they say "you" (familiar)?
12. Name two common foods eaten by "Ticos"?
13. Bring a platano back with you.
14. Draw a map to the museum on the back of this paper.

Sharing your Testimony

It is a given that at some point you will be asked to "testify" about what God has been doing in your life or who He is to you. This can be a very powerful and positive moment if you are ready, or it can be a disaster if you're not. Doing this in a cross-cultural situation and through a translator can be tricky. The following are some things to think about.

Pray—Start by talking to the ONE that you intend to talk about before you do any talking at all. Trust that He will help you to say what He would like you to say.

Choose your words wisely—Think about how certain words will prompt feelings, even if you disagree with the interpretation others have of what you are saying. Should you call yourself a crusader when your audience knows crusaders as invaders? Should you even use the term Christian in a country that has seen wars between political Christians and Muslims or among those who think being born in a certain country automatically makes you a Christian? The word has so much meaning to some people that you might want to talk about what makes you a Christian, your relationship with Christ, rather than what you call yourself.

Christian "church talk"—avoid it!—Being "born into a Christian home" may be understood by your non-U.S. audience as something very different from what you mean, such as you were born in a house, not in a hospital. It can also be confusing—how can a building be "Christian"? Being "born again" could take some real explaining... are you ready to do that? Or do you want to share your testimony in simpler terms?

Talk about Jesus, not your church or Christianity—Most other countries' peoples are extremely relational, which is to say our testimony should come across the same way—as our being extremely relational to Jesus. Make Him the center as though He is standing next to you and you are simply telling people about Him and your journey with Him.

A testimony is more than your conversion—Many people think that a testimony is telling people about your conversion. That is certainly part of your testimony, but it may be more pertinent to talk about what has been happening between you and Jesus in the recent past or even this morning.

Be real—If you struggle, say it. Don't sugarcoat your journey with Jesus. Following Jesus is hard. He seems to use that difficulty to teach us.

Prepare—Write out a testimony. Rehearse it. Say it to others several times. You should know it, not read it, but by rehearsing it you will do better when you get in front of a crowd.

Exercise in Writing your Testimony

Pray about a time you have had with Jesus that was meaningful to you. Think it through. Is this what would glorify Jesus and arouse interest in your audience? Write out the following on a separate sheet of paper, filling in and elaborating.

Hi, my name is _____

[It may sound odd, but many people forget to say their name]

One time when I was_____ years old

I was _____

With _____

Doing _____

When _____happened

This made me feel or did _____to me

People around me responded by
doing/saying_____

I thought about Jesus because_____

I asked Jesus to_____

What happened next was_____

Because of what happened with Jesus I'm now _____

Exercise in "Thinking Through" Your Experiences with Jesus

Pray about how you think of your faith. Focus on how you know the risen Jesus, instead of focusing on a "club" called Christianity that you belong to. Think in terms of relationship as you explore the following questions:

If you wanted to introduce your best friend to someone, what things would you say about this person?

_____

What does Jesus mean to you?

_____

What have been your most recent experiences with Jesus, our Holy Spirit and our Father God?

_____

Has He recently helped you through a tough time?

_____

Has He recently taught you something new (and whether it was a hard-learned lesson)?

_____

Has he touched you in a way that let you know He was close?

_____

What has His word (scripture) been saying to you?

_____

Have there been some answered prayers lately?

_____

Encouraging Each Other

How you relate to each other is one of the most powerful witnesses you and your team will have. Imagine your host country partners having just spent the day watching your team fighting with each other, making fun of each other, and cutting each other down—then listening to you that night trying to convince them that they need what you have. They would think, "Why would we want to be like them?"

To avoid these negative group dynamics, strive to build each other up. Foster this attitude by creating an environment where positive statements are thrown out like verbal candy. An oft-repeated saying is that it takes nine positives to equal the effect of one negative comment. Whether that's exactly true or not, the basic principal is accurate in our experience. This means everyone should use every opportunity to encourage others in the group.

Look for ways to affirm the growth you see in your team members, to thank them for their contributions and unique gifts, and to inspire them when they face challenges. Start doing this before the trip begins and continue throughout the trip. To help you in your role as an encourager, we have gathered some ideas for encouraging your group.

- Make your compliments specific and detailed when you can. "I like the way you kept smiling when it got tough" is more effective than "great job." But don't withhold a "great job" trying to think of something more to say.

- Timing can make a compliment effective—a "great job" said at the right moment, just as something was done, is specific and highly effective.

- Pray for your team members (even those whose personalities may be most difficult to work with).

Guide to Team Devotions

Keeping centered around Jesus is the primary goal of every short-term mission group. This guide provides two weeks of helpful passages regarding service and some of the circumstances that short-term mission teams typically encounter. Please use this to help you plan your devotions with the group. The first set of topics is on servanthood, the second on spiritual warfare (Armor of God).

Servanthood Devotions

Day 1: Ephesians 4: 1–6, Living with each other. It isn't easy to live with many different personalities in unusual circumstances for a week. How can we work together as a team? Protect relationships? One of our biggest witnesses is how we live with each other. What are some creative ways that you can think of to encourage and support each other during the trip?

Day 2: Matthew 14: 22–34 (concentrate on 22–24 today), Facing Difficult Circumstances. Difficulty is going to occur. You are going to encounter a different language, different culture, different food, and different personalities. Grow from it (James 1:2–4). What challenges might you expect on a trip like this?

Day 3: Matthew 14: 22–34 (concentrate on 25–27 today), What are your Fears? What are some of your expectations and fears for this trip? We can take courage that we are walking through this with Christ at our side. "Take Courage! It is I. Don't be afraid!" What reasons do we have for "taking courage?"

Day 4: Matthew 14: 22–34 (concentrate on 27–31 today), Taking a Risk. What risks can you take on the trip? When you go home? Remember that Christ is reaching out his hand and asking us to step out of the boat (to take a risk) just as he did with Peter. What a great challenge and opportunity! Think of what the other disciples missed out on by refusing to step out in faith.

Day 5: Matthew 14: 22–34 (concentrate on 32 today), God is in Control. He is the Son of God. He controls the wind and waves. We can put our trust and confidence in him as provider and strength, but sometimes it is difficult to turn complete control of our lives over to Him. What are some of the areas that you might need to leave in His care or in His control?

Day 6: Matthew 8:1–13, Touching the Untouchables. It is easy to care for the lovable. What about the unlovable, the untouchables? Who are the people who are most difficult for you to reach out and love? Remember that for many we may be the only physical manifestation of Christ that they may ever meet. Strategize how you might touch those who are difficult to love.

Day 7: Debriefing John 15: 9–17, Love one Another: Going from a Servant to a Friend. A true friend is one who goes beyond serving to *knowing* a person. You have had a great opportunity to reach out and share with others—sometimes it is easier with those you don't know. Now, what about those we do know? How can you become "friends" to those at home?

Other Servanthood Passages & Topics

Mathew 5:1–12	What Qualities will be Blessed?
Mathew 16:24–28	The Cost of Following Christ's Example
Mathew 18:1–6	Humility: The Key to Servanthood
Mathew 20:20–28	Who is Greater in the Kingdom?
John 10:1–18	The Shepherd and the Sheep
John 13:5–20	Washing the Feet of the Disciples

Armor of God Devotions

Your team is going into hostile territory and fighting against a devious enemy. The following passages and reflections from the book of Ephesians give you the different pieces of armor that you will need to dress you for battle.

Day 1: Ephesians 6: 10–20, The Armor of God. We may start to "struggle" as a group (v12) without any clear idea why. Tensions fly, attitudes sour, obstacles appear, and solutions fail. Could it be you're up against "the schemes of the devil"? Paul encourages us to "put on the full armor of God," not just a single piece. What are the elements of armor Paul lists for us? What are their functions? Look at the names of the armor... don't they also describe Jesus? How does it make you feel that you can dress in Jesus every day? Where does the power really come from as we meet "the schemes of the devil"? Are you completely dressed today?

Day 2: Ephesians 6: 14a, The Armored Belt of Truth. How can dressing in the belt of Truth make a difference? Is it possible that you are functioning with a mindset that is not completely true? Are you standing firm in Jesus' strength or in your own? Perhaps you are struggling against situations that are really "spiritual" rather than "flesh and blood." What thoughts may be going through your mind that aren't true: Have you thought, "I don't have the strength to do this or that" when scripture says, "I can do all things through Him who strengthens me" (Ph 4:13). Anything the enemy can do to distract us from the pure truth and power of Jesus can set us up for a fall. Verse 12 talks about who our real enemy is. Are you acting on the truth?

Day 3: Ephesians 6:14b, The Breastplate of Righteousness. The Breastplate covers our heart, the center of who we are in Jesus now that He resides in us (Jn 14:17–20). Our hearts are good not because of anything we've done but because of Jesus. How often have you felt that you were bad? Could that be an assault from the enemy? Your righteousness or goodness is Jesus' righteousness and goodness. That is the place you serve from... you actually give Jesus away. Are you protecting your heart? Is His protection in place? How is your heart today?

Day 4: Ephesians 6:15a, Shoes to Stand in the Gospel. Nothing is more solid than standing on the Rock. Nothing gives more peace than seeing the big picture from a place like the Rock. The Gospel is like that... it gives firmness and peace. Isn't that why you're on this trip? People who lack Jesus are dying around us. Are we quick-footed enough to respond? What is the Gospel to you? What would motive you to share Him? Do you feel confident and ready to share Him? In what ways can you share Him on this trip?

Day 5: Ephesians 6:16a, The Shield of Faith. Faith in Jesus is a shield. What kind of flaming arrows has the enemy been flinging your way? Our faith in Jesus simply extinguishes those arrows. How do you use the shield... defense only? Could it be for offense too? Can we wield the shield on other's behalf?

Day 6: Ephesians 6:17, The Helmet of Salvation. Have you ever doubted your salvation? Maybe your helmet is not securely on. It's an area where the enemy would like to land a fiery arrow. There is another angle: with our heads we made a decision to live for Jesus... to give our very lives to Jesus... that's where it all started. What difference does that make in your life? How about in the lives of others around you?

Day 7: Ephesians 6:17b, The Sword of the Spirit: the Word of God. This is a weapon of offense... cutting the lies, chasing the enemy away, and killing the thoughts the enemy has planted. But it's double-edged: it can also give life, heal the wounded and sick and guide us further down His path. It does nothing unless grasped and used. A sword that hangs on the wall or stays on the bookshelf is no threat to the enemy nor encouragement to live by. Where is your sword? How can you use it against the evil one? How can you use it to produce life in Jesus?

Journaling

If you are like most travelers abroad, you will find a lot can happen in a short time. It is easy to become overwhelmed and stop processing, much less remember the richness of the experience years later. Journaling can be an invaluable tool, for memory and for engaging with the experience to create deeper insights, beyond observation. Even a few minutes a day, writing down some notes on what you found to be humorous, exciting, unique, and challenging will help you to relive the experience and give you some great stories to share at home. The next pages provide a place for a trip journal. Some starter questions to get you writing:

- What unique customs did you encounter?
- What interesting foods did you enjoy the most? Find most challenging?
- What did you notice that's different about their culture from your own?
- What types of activities did the people spend their free time doing?
- What was their worship like?
- What did you learn in their language?
- What humorous anecdotes or fun stories did you experience?
- What did you find most challenging living in this culture?
- What passages or Biblical truths did you learn or grow from on the trip?
- What perspectives did you gain on your life back home?

Team Journaling and Shared Journaling

You may choose to keep the journal private or share it with a different group member or two each evening and invite them to add their thoughts in "Guest comments." This can stimulate each person's own journaling, seed your group discussions, and give you an interesting "book" to distribute at the end of the trip.

Trip Journal	Date	Location

Things I learned today:

A truth or scripture I found especially helpful or insightful:

Meaningful observations, stories, or experiences:

Guest Observations today (may be on different subjects from those above) or Comments:

Trip Journal	Date	Location

Things I learned today:

A truth or scripture I found especially helpful or insightful:

Meaningful observations, stories, or experiences:

Guest Observations today (may be on different subjects from those above) or Comments:

Trip Journal	Date	Location

Things I learned today:

A truth or scripture I found especially helpful or insightful:

Meaningful observations, stories, or experiences:

Guest Observations today (may be on different subjects from those above) or Comments:

Trip Journal	Date	Location

Things I learned today:

A truth or scripture I found especially helpful or insightful:

Meaningful observations, stories, or experiences:

Guest Observations today (may be on different subjects from those above) or Comments:

Trip Journal	Date	Location

Things I learned today:

A truth or scripture I found especially helpful or insightful:

Meaningful observations, stories, or experiences:

Guest Observations today (may be on different subjects from those above) or Comments:

Trip Journal | Date | Location

Things I learned today:

A truth or scripture I found especially helpful or insightful:

Meaningful observations, stories, or experiences:

Guest Observations today (may be on different subjects from those above) or Comments:

Trip Journal	Date	Location

Things I learned today:

A truth or scripture I found especially helpful or insightful:

Meaningful observations, stories, or experiences:

Guest Observations today (may be on different subjects from those above) or Comments:

Trip Journal

| Date | Location |

Things I learned today:

A truth or scripture I found especially helpful or insightful:

Meaningful observations, stories, or experiences:

Guest Observations today (may be on different subjects from those above) or Comments:

Trip Journal	Date	Location

Things I learned today:

A truth or scripture I found especially helpful or insightful:

Meaningful observations, stories, or experiences:

Guest Observations today (may be on different subjects from those above) or Comments:

Trip Journal	Date	Location

Things I learned today:

A truth or scripture I found especially helpful or insightful:

Meaningful observations, stories, or experiences:

Guest Observations today (may be on different subjects from those above) or Comments:

Trip Journal	Date	Location

Things I learned today:

A truth or scripture I found especially helpful or insightful:

Meaningful observations, stories, or experiences:

Guest Observations today (may be on different subjects from those above) or Comments:

Trip Journal

Date	Location

Things I learned today:

A truth or scripture I found especially helpful or insightful:

Meaningful observations, stories, or experiences:

Guest Observations today (may be on different subjects from those above) or Comments:

Trip Journal	Date	Location

Things I learned today:

A truth or scripture I found especially helpful or insightful:

Meaningful observations, stories, or experiences:

Guest Observations today (may be on different subjects from those above) or Comments:

Trip Journal	Date	Location

Things I learned today:

A truth or scripture I found especially helpful or insightful:

Meaningful observations, stories, or experiences:

Guest Observations today (may be on different subjects from those above) or Comments:

Debriefing

A debriefing is a way for individuals to gain the most from the mission experience. Your leader must decide to do this as a group. Psychological debriefing developed as a group technique to address traumatic events. It gives those who have experienced something unusual a chance to share their observations and feelings. The participants can then better understand what has happened.

The technique has a sound grounding in the science of how we form memories and develop insights—it should not be dismissed as a "touchy-feely" exercise that has no real benefit. Teachers sometimes use a similar technique after a classroom activity. A debriefing can be a unique opportunity for learning and spiritual growth.

While a mission trip is not like losing your home in a hurricane—we hope—it has likely presented the group with stress, both good and bad, and changed who they are in some way. The debriefing helps trip participants make sense of what the trip means to them and their spirituality. Without the debriefing, a person might be on the brink of a positive change from the experience and not engage with it enough to realize a change. The trip fails to have its full effect, and sometimes any effect. Debriefing can be that important.

What the Debriefing is NOT!

- The debriefing is not a gripe session.
- The debriefing is not open season for assigning blame.

When griping and blaming start becoming the focus the leader should assume an authoritative role and redirect the discussion, reminding the people that this is an exercise in learning, not in complaining or blaming.

The debriefing sets the stage for how the trip experience will continue to teach you over your lifetime. It does not mean that everything the trip will teach will be learned at the debriefing. The debriefing can plant seeds that will grow over time. These seeds may not form at all if the fresh experiences are not thought over and shared shortly after the experience.

Debriefings for Mission Trips have Four Components

Facts. What happened on the trip. This is different for each person, and the leaders should keep in mind that "what happened" is more than what the leaders saw. If there are 12 trip participants, there are 12 accounts of what happened.

Reactions. What you felt or did when something happened.

Meaning. What you learned. How the experience fits into your spirituality. How you will describe it to others.

Reentry. Reentry is a discussion of some challenges you may face with the trip ending and the return home.

Your group leader would facilitate a debriefing meeting. The *Footsteps Short-Term Missions Leadership Handbook* has detailed instructions for your leader on how to facilitate a successful debriefing. The following form on pages 84 to 86 can be used to prepare for the debriefing—your leader may have you do other things instead or in addition.

If your leader isn't using the *Leadership Handbook* or the group can't get together for a debriefing, the following form can help you do some debriefing work on your own. This includes engaging with your experience, forming meaning out of it, and integrating the new experience into the life you return to. Yes, that sounds like a tall order to do with a simple form. That's why we strongly recommend a debriefing meeting facilitated by your group leader. A formal debriefing lets you benefit from others in the group, in the debriefing and afterwards. It includes reentry plans for your group to continue bonds that may have grown on the trip and to grow new bonds among team members from looking back at the shared experience.

Debriefing Form

What did you learn from the trip?

What were some highlights?

Debriefing Form (continued)

Reentry

<u>Mountaintop & Valleys</u>- You have been part of an incredible group of servants. You have met new friends and established new relationships. Understand the natural tendency to have a letdown upon your return.

<u>Things to Watch Out For</u> [write notes from discussion or, if working on your own, write down your thoughts on these items]
1. Stomach Problems

2. Jet Lag

3. Shift from a Family to Individual Mentality

4. Be Careful of Spontaneous Decisions

5. Expect Muted Enthusiasm from People at Home

6. Reverse Culture Shock

Debriefing Form (continued)

The Trip is not Over
Satan can attack as much after as during or before a trip.

What are you going to do with what you have learned from this trip? Think about it, pray about it. Consider how the experience helped you see outside your usual existence. If it didn't do this, why didn't it?

John 15:9–17
Key to Passage: I no longer call you servants, because a servant does not know his master's business. Instead, I have called you friends, for everything I have learned from the Father I have made known to you [write notes from discussion or, if working on your own, write down your thoughts on this passage in relation to your trip]

Positives (Encouragements). Continue to find ways to encourage others on your team (including your leader) especially during this time that can be a little depressing. [write notes from discussion or, if working on your own, your thoughts and possible actions]

Share with your Church, Community, & Partners

Recapping the Trip. Upon your return, it can reinforce good feelings to share the trip with those who helped make it happen. The following are ideas how to do this effectively:

- **Dinner or Dessert**. Prepare a dinner or dessert of food typical of the host country and share some pictures.

- **Give a gift**. Write a thank you note or card to those who supported you in prayer or with financial gifts or go a step further and bring them a small gift from the country (e.g., a bag of coffee from Costa Rica, vanilla from Mexico, a small wooden carving from Africa).

- **Picture Website**. Put your pictures on a website and let your partners know the website address.

Warning: Don't overwhelm your partners with too much. Let them ask to hear more. Share a small picture book (15 pictures max) or one small story when they ask how the trip went. If they want to hear more, you can give more detail or set up a time to share more of the trip.

Music Aids

Chords and Keys for Guitar and Keyboard

Have you ever wondered how a band plays together when all the leader says is "in the key of A"? This section helps you with this and more. The tools can help your group perform music, together or with local people. They help them communicate about the music they are trying to play. The tools assume those using them can play an instrument or sing already.

You may have people in your group of varying musical backgrounds. For example, you may have a good piano player who can sight-read music but your guitar player may be a beginner who knows only a few chord groups. These tools can help them bridge their gap in skills to play together. Your local partners may have different ways of notating music and language differences can get in the way. Many countries will use the SOLFEGE system for music, for example, while in the United States we are more used to using the ABCDEFG notation system. The following tools can help. (See a detailed explanation of SOLFEGE on page 114).

> After hours and hours on a plane and driving through the mud and rain and fighting off bugs, you unexpectedly find you are responsible for music in the church service that night—and you are so tired you cannot remember a chord or chord progression. Luckily, you have this handy music tool...

This section provides both basic aids (how to play primary chords in different keys) and more advanced aids (additional chords for more challenging music). You will find the chord listed for guitar, and directly underneath it, the chord on the piano in its root position, so you can compare the two and follow someone else playing the alternate instrument. This guide can help when a musician in your group needs to do the following:

- Easily transpose a song that is too high or too low for the singers in your group

- Figure out the chords for a song that you know the words to but can't remember the chords

- Provide the typical chords used in a key so you can easily jam with locals and learn some of their music

- Help you to follow along with another musician and compare what chords they are playing—the pictorial guide allows you to see at a glance what key a guitar player or piano player is using, even if you don't know how to play the other instrument.

- Help during practice to learn chords in a specific key

Primary Chords for Major Keys

Music is very mathematical: certain chords are associated with each key with mathematical regularity. The following pages help you to learn these associations. They provide pictures of how to play the chords in each key on guitar and piano. In these pictures, we show the finger positions on the strings or the keys with numbers. The white numbers below correspond to the guitar fingering and the black numbers correspond to the piano fingering.

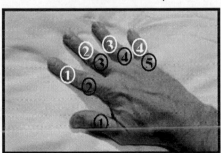

We have listed the primary major chords and the minor chords. We also provide the Solfege equivalent, the number of sharps or flats, and some more challenging chords for advanced musicians.

Key of Ab

Primary Chords

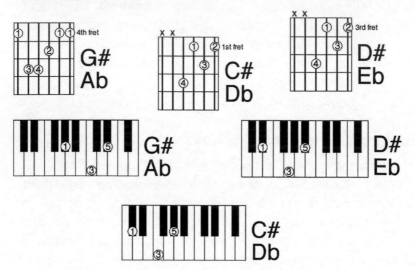

Solfege: LE or SI, 4 flats—Bb, Eb, Ab, Db

Minor Chords

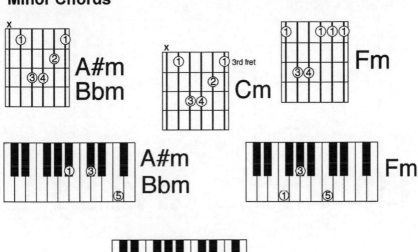

Advanced Chords: Dbmaj7, Gdim

Key of A

Primary Chords

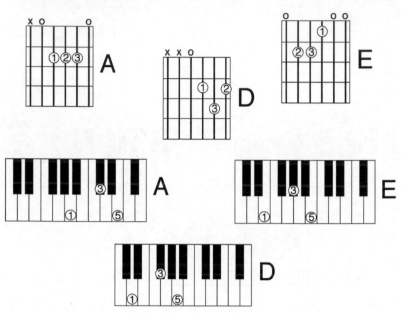

Solfege: LA,   3 sharps—F#, C#, G#

Minor Chords

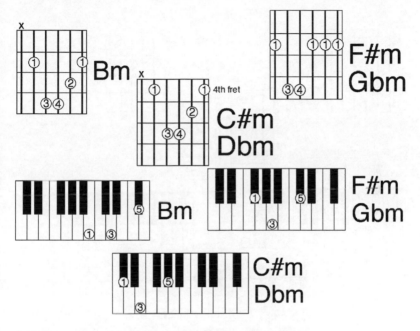

Advanced Chords: Dmaj7, G#dim

Key of Bb

Primary Chords

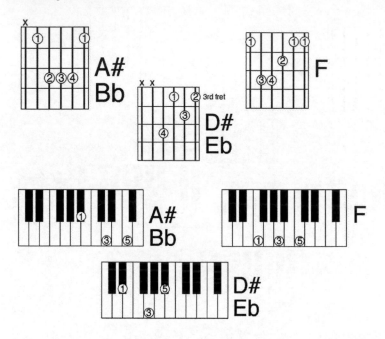

Solfege: TE or LI, 2 flats—Bb & Eb

Minor Chords

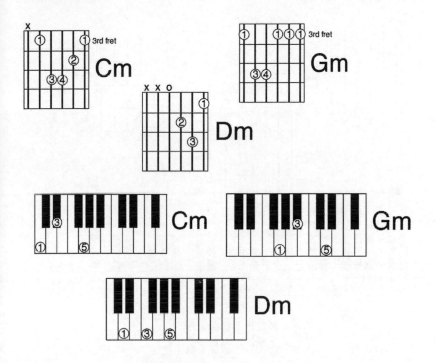

Advanced Chords: Ebmaj7, Adim

Key of B

Primary Chords

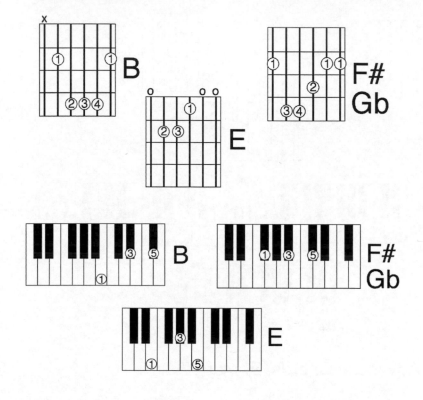

Solfege: TI, 5 sharps—F#, C#, G#, D#, A#

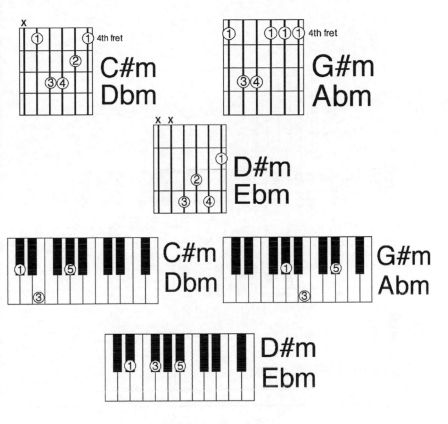

Minor Chords

C#m
Dbm

G#m
Abm

D#m
Ebm

C#m
Dbm

G#m
Abm

D#m
Ebm

Advanced Chords: Emaj7, A#dim

Key of C

Primary Chords

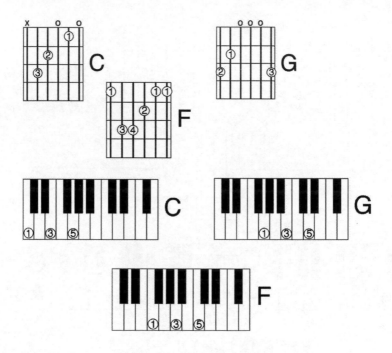

Solfege: DO, No flats or sharps

Minor Chords

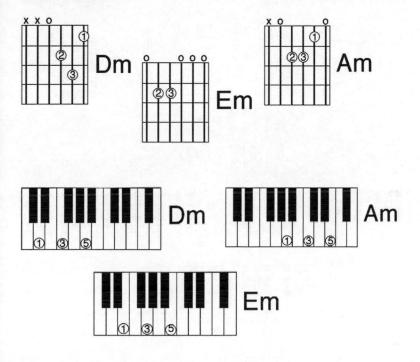

Advanced Chords: Fmaj7, Bdim

Key of Db

Primary Chords

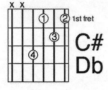
C#
Db

F#
Gb

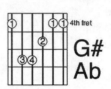
G#
Ab

C#
Db

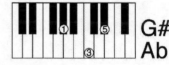
G#
Ab

F#
Gb

Solfege: RA or DI, 5 flats— Bb, Eb, Ab, Db, Gb

Minor Chords

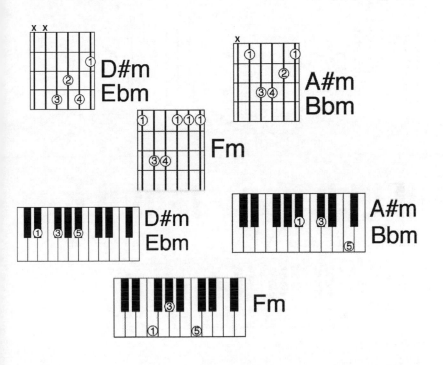

Advanced Chords: Gbmaj7, Cdim

Key of D

Primary Chords

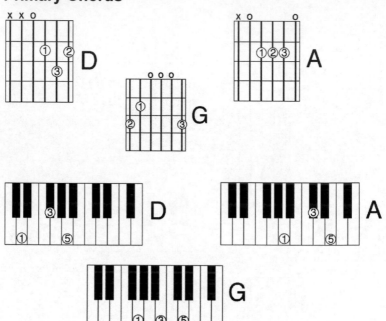

Solfege: RE, 2 sharps—F# & C#

Minor Chords

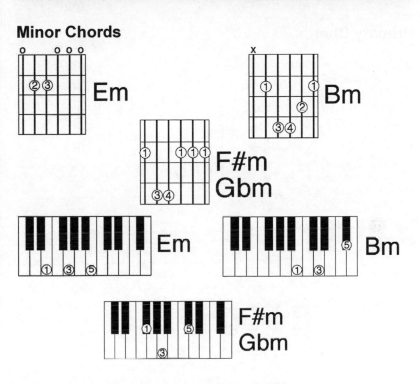

Advanced Chords: Gmaj7, C#dim

Key of Eb

Primary Chords

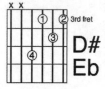

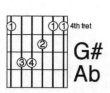

Solfege: ME or RI, 3 flats—Bb, Eb, Ab

Minor Chords

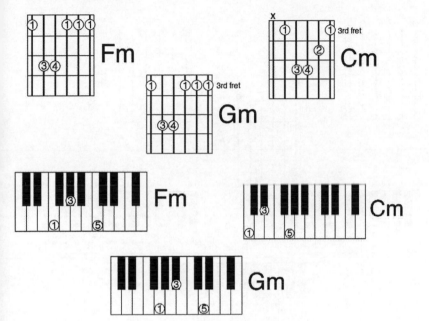

Advanced Chords: Abmaj7, Ddim

Key of E

Primary Chords

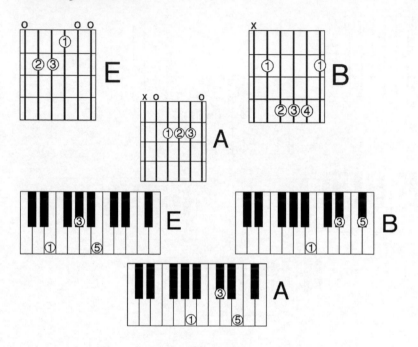

Solfege: MI, 4 sharps—F#, C#, G#, D#

Minor Chords

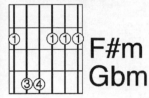 F#m
Gbm

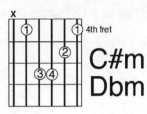 C#m
Dbm

 G#m
Abm

 F#m
Gbm

 C#m
Dbm

 G#m
Abm

Advanced Chords: Amaj7, D#dim

Key of F

Primary Chords

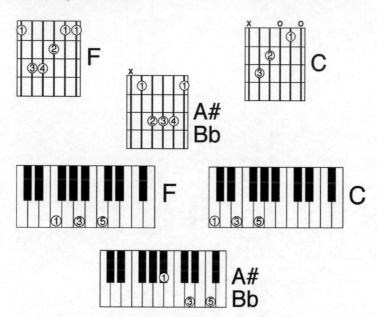

Solfege: FA, 1 flat—Bb

Minor Chords

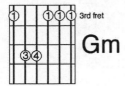 Gm

 Am

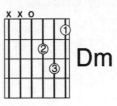 Dm

 Gm

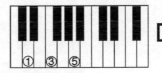 Dm

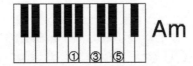 Am

Advanced Chords: Bbmaj7, Edim

Key of Gb or F#

Primary Chords

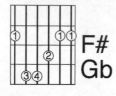  **F#**
Gb

 B

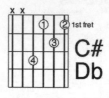 **C#**
Db

 **F#**
Gb

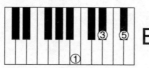 **C#**
Db

B

Solfege: SE or FI 6 flats or 6 sharps—Bb, Eb, Ab, Db, Gb, Cb or F#, C#, G#, D#, A#, E#

Minor Chords

 G#m Abm

 A#m Bbm

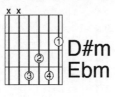 D#m Ebm

 G#m Abm

 D#m Ebm

 A#m Bbm

Advanced Chords: Bmaj7, Fdim

Key of G

Primary Chords

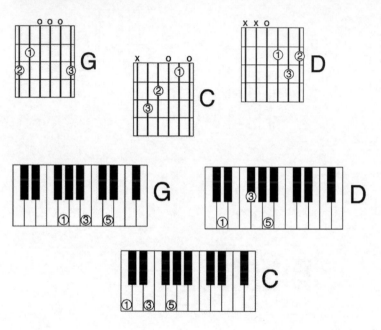

Solfege: SO, 1 sharp—F#

Minor Chords

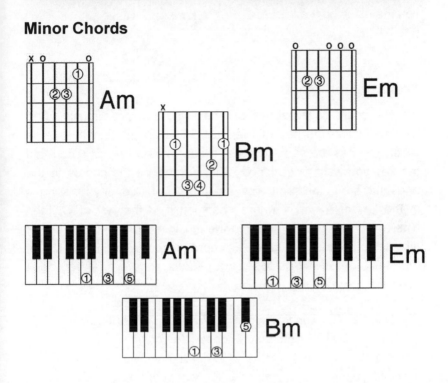

Advanced Chords: Cmaj7, F#dim

Guitar Notes for Tuning

To the right, the diagram gives you the notes on the frets for the guitar.

Transposing Music

The chord pages above can help you transpose music. Start by determining the key of the music you are playing by seeing which key has the same chords in your musical piece. Then find the key you want to transpose to, and change the chords to the ones that are in the same position in that key (e.g., if your song is in the key of A and you are changing it to the key of C, then wherever there is a "D" chord in the music (second chord in key of A) you would change it to an "F" chord (second chord in the key of C). This tool allows you to learn to play a song even if you don't have a chord chart.

> Advanced Tip: For keyboard players who would like to add a little variety, you can change the positioning of the notes that you play on the piano—for example, for the "C" chord instead of playing C, E, G, you could play E, G, C or G, C, E in this order. The musical term for this type of variation is an "inversion."

Solfege—Another way of writing chords, common outside the United States

You may find yourself in another country wanting to play with some local musicians. You ask them for music and they give you a chart with chords, but it doesn't don't look like anything you've seen before. They are likely using a different representation for chords called Solfege. The good thing is it is easy to convert to our chord names.

Instead of chord representations using our alphabet (A, B, C, D, E, F, G), Solfa (or solfege) represents either the pitch or the relationship between pitches found in music. These are DO, RE, MI, FA, SO, LA, TI, & another DO that is one octave higher than the first. You may recall these from the well known song in the "Sound of Music."

Solfa can be used two ways. It can be used as a moveable system (sometimes called Tonic Solfa) where each symbol represents a relationship to the other pitches. In other words, FA would be three pitches higher than DO. DO or any other symbol can be any pitch or note in this usage.

Solfa can also be used as fixed pitches where DO is always the pitch "C". This is typically what you would see if your friends from the other country gave you a chord chart. Here is an easy conversion chart to help you determine the differences.

C	D	E	F	G	A	B
DO	RE	MI	FA	SO	LA	TI

What about sharps and flats?

Sharps and flats have their own lesser-known Solfege names based on moving up (sharp) or down (flat) the scales. The following chart lists these equivalent conversions.

Ascending Chromatic Scale (by sharps)
DO DI RE RI MI FA FI SO SI LA LI TI DO

Descending Chromatic Scale (by flats)
DO TI TE LA LE SO SE FA MI ME RE RA DO

C	C#/Db	D	D#/Eb	E	F	F#/Gb	G	G#/Ab	A	A#/Bb	B
DO	DI/RA	RE	RI/ME	MI	FA	FI/SE	SO	SI/LE	LA	LI/TE	TI

Address Book

Each person you meet is an opportunity for you both to learn from each other, encourage each other, and grow together. Fostering relationships after the trip can bear rich fruit. The following pages help you collect contact information.

Addresses

Name	
Address	
Email Address	
Telephone #	Alternate Telephone #
Birth date	

Name	
Address	
Email Address	
Telephone #	Alternate Telephone #
Birth date	

Name	
Address	
Email Address	
Telephone #	Alternate Telephone #
Birth date	

Name	
Address	
Email Address	
Telephone #	Alternate Telephone #
Birth date	

Name	
Address	
Email Address	
Telephone #	Alternate Telephone #
Birth date	

Name	
Address	
Email Address	
Telephone #	Alternate Telephone #
Birth date	

Name	
Address	
Email Address	
Telephone #	Alternate Telephone #
Birth date	

Name	
Address	
Email Address	
Telephone #	Alternate Telephone #
Birth date	

Name	
Address	
Email Address	
Telephone #	Alternate Telephone #
Birth date	

Name	
Address	
Email Address	
Telephone #	Alternate Telephone #
Birth date	

Name	
Address	
Email Address	
Telephone #	Alternate Telephone #
Birth date	

Name	
Address	
Email Address	
Telephone #	Alternate Telephone #
Birth date	

Name	
Address	
Email Address	
Telephone #	Alternate Telephone #
Birth date	

Name	
Address	
Email Address	
Telephone #	Alternate Telephone #
Birth date	

Name	
Address	
Email Address	
Telephone #	Alternate Telephone #
Birth date	

Name	
Address	
Email Address	
Telephone #	Alternate Telephone #
Birth date	

Name	
Address	
Email Address	
Telephone #	Alternate Telephone #
Birth date	

Name	
Address	
Email Address	
Telephone #	Alternate Telephone #
Birth date	

Name	
Address	
Email Address	
Telephone #	Alternate Telephone #
Birth date	

Name	
Address	
Email Address	
Telephone #	Alternate Telephone #
Birth date	

Name	
Address	
Email Address	
Telephone #	Alternate Telephone #
Birth date	

Name	
Address	
Email Address	
Telephone #	Alternate Telephone #
Birth date	

Name	
Address	
Email Address	
Telephone #	Alternate Telephone #
Birth date	

Name	
Address	
Email Address	
Telephone #	Alternate Telephone #
Birth date	

Name	
Address	
Email Address	
Telephone #	Alternate Telephone #
Birth date	

Name	
Address	
Email Address	
Telephone #	Alternate Telephone #
Birth date	

Name	
Address	
Email Address	
Telephone #	Alternate Telephone #
Birth date	

Name	
Address	
Email Address	
Telephone #	Alternate Telephone #
Birth date	

Name	
Address	
Email Address	
Telephone #	Alternate Telephone #
Birth date	

Communication Cards

Fill in the sections below, tear them off, and give them to a friend

Name	
Address	
Email Address	
Telephone #	Alternate Telephone #

Name	
Address	
Email Address	
Telephone #	Alternate Telephone #

Name	
Address	
Email Address	
Telephone #	Alternate Telephone #

Name	
Address	
Email Address	
Telephone #	Alternate Telephone #

Name	
Address	
Email Address	
Telephone #	Alternate Telephone #

Name	
Address	
Email Address	
Telephone #	Alternate Telephone #

Name	
Address	
Email Address	
Telephone #	Alternate Telephone #

Name	
Address	
Email Address	
Telephone #	Alternate Telephone #

Name	
Address	
Email Address	
Telephone #	Alternate Telephone #

Name	
Address	
Email Address	
Telephone #	Alternate Telephone #

Name	
Address	
Email Address	
Telephone #	Alternate Telephone #

Name	
Address	
Email Address	
Telephone #	Alternate Telephone #

Name	
Address	
Email Address	
Telephone #	Alternate Telephone #

Name	
Address	
Email Address	
Telephone #	Alternate Telephone #

Name	
Address	
Email Address	
Telephone #	Alternate Telephone #

Name	
Address	
Email Address	
Telephone #	Alternate Telephone #

Name	
Address	
Email Address	
Telephone #	Alternate Telephone #

Name	
Address	
Email Address	
Telephone #	Alternate Telephone #

Partner Communication Center

Many of you have people praying, supporting, and encouraging you as partners on your service trip. Here is an easy place to record their information so you can keep in touch before, during, and after trip either by writing an email, sending some pictures over the Internet, writing a postcard, or just thanking them for being part of your trip.

Name	
Address	
Email Address	
Telephone #	Alternate Telephone #
How he/she has helped:	
Thank you sent?	

Name	
Address	
Email Address	
Telephone #	Alternate Telephone #
How he/she has helped:	
Thank you sent?	

Name	
Address	
Email Address	
Telephone #	Alternate Telephone #
How he/she has helped:	
Thank you sent?	

Name	
Address	
Email Address	
Telephone #	Alternate Telephone #
How he/she has helped:	
Thank you sent?	

Name	
Address	
Email Address	
Telephone #	Alternate Telephone #
How he/she has helped:	
Thank you sent?	

Name	
Address	
Email Address	
Telephone #	Alternate Telephone #
How he/she has helped:	
Thank you sent?	

Name	
Address	
Email Address	
Telephone #	Alternate Telephone #
How he/she has helped:	
Thank you sent?	

Appendices

Time Zones (Time +/- Hours from Eastern Standard Time)

Addis Ababa, Ethiopia	+ 8	La Paz, Bolivia	+ 1
Alexandria, Egypt	+ 7	Liverpool, England	+ 5
Algiers, Algeria	+ 6	London, England	+ 5
Amsterdam, Netherlands	+ 6	Madrid, Spain	+ 6
Athens, Greece	+ 7	Manila, Philippines	+ 13
Auckland, New Zealand	+ 17	Mecca, Saudi Arabia	+ 8
Azores Island, Portugal	+ 4	Melbourne, Australia	+ 15
Baghdad, Iraq	+ 8	Mexico City, Mexico	− 1
Bangkok, Thailand	+ 12	Montevideo, Uruguay	+ 2
Beijing, China	+ 13	Montreal, QU Canada	+ 0
Belfast, N. Ireland, UK	+ 5	Moscow, Russia	+ 8
Belgrade, Serbia	+ 6	Nagasaki, Japan	+ 14
Berlin, Germany	+ 6	Nairobi, Kenya	+ 8
Bogota, Columbia	+ 0	Oslo, Norway	+ 6
Bombay, India	+ 10:30	Panama, Panama	+ 0
Bremen, Germany	+ 6	Paris, France	+ 6
Brisbane, Australia	+ 15	Perth, Australia	+ 13
Brussels, Belgium	+ 6	Papua New Guinea	+ 15
Bucharest, Romania	+ 7	Prague, Czech Republic	+ 6
Budapest, Hungary	+ 6	Quito, Ecuador	+ 0
Buenos Aires, Argentina	+ 2	Regina, SA Canada	− 1
Cairo, Egypt	+ 7	Reykjavik, Iceland	+ 5
Calcutta, India	+ 10:30	Rio de Janeiro, Brazil	+ 2
Cape Town, South Africa	+ 7	Rome, Italy	+ 6
Caracas, Venezuela	+ 1	Santiago, Chile	+ 1
Casablanca, Morocco	+ 5	Seoul, South Korea	+ 14
Copenhagen, Denmark	+ 6	Shanghai, China	+ 13
Dawson, YT Canada	− 3	Shannon, Ireland	+ 5
Dakar, Senegal	+ 5	Singapore, Singapore	+ 13
Delhi, India	+ 10:30	St. Johns NF Canada	+ 1:30
Dhaka, Bangladesh	+ 13	St. Petersburg, Russia	+ 8
Dublin, Ireland	+ 5	Stockholm, Sweden	+ 6
Edmonton, AL Canada	− 2	Sydney, Australia	+ 15
Gdansk, Poland	+ 6	Tashkent, Uzbekistan	+ 11
Geneva, Switzerland	+ 6	Tehran, Iran	+ 8:30
Guam, US Territory	+ 15	Tokyo, Japan	+ 14
Havana, Cuba	+ 0	Toronto, OT Canada	+ 0
Helsinki, Finland	+ 7	Ulaanbaatar, Mongolia	+ 13
Ho Chi Minh, Vietnam	+ 12	Valparaiso, Chile	+ 1
Hong Kong, China	+ 13	Vancouver, BC Canada	− 3
Honolulu, Hawaii US	− 5	Vladivostok, Russia	+ 15
Istanbul, Turkey	+ 7	Vienna, Austria	+ 6
Jakarta, Indonesia	+ 12	Warsaw, Poland	+ 6
Jerusalem, Israel	+ 7	Wellington, New Zealand	+ 17
Jeddah, Saudi Arabia	+ 8	Yangon, Myanmar	+ 11:30
Johannesburg, South Africa	+ 7	Yokohama, Japan	+ 14
Juneau, Alaska, US	− 4	Zurich, Switzerland	+ 6
Karachi, Pakistan	+ 10	US Central Standard	− 1
Lima, Peru	+ 0	US Mountain Standard	− 2
Lisbon, Portugal	+ 5	US Pacific Standard	− 3

24-Hour Clock Conversion Sheet

Much of the world measures time with a 24-hour clock, rather than using a.m. and p.m. as we typically do in the United States. In the United States, we call the 24-hour time "military time" because the U.S. military uses it. In other countries, that term might not make sense because everyone, not just the military, uses that terminology. The following is a handy chart for when you are tired and not quite sure if 1800 hours is 6 p.m. or 7 p.m.

Standard	24-Hour	Standard	24-Hour
12 midnight	2400	12 noon	1200
12:01 am	0001	12:01 pm	1201
12:15 am	0015	12:15 pm	1215
12:30 am	0030	12.30 pm	1230
12:45 am	0045	12:45 pm	1245
1 am	0100	1 pm	1300
2 am	0200	2 pm	1400
3 am	0300	3 pm	1500
4 am	0400	4 pm	1600
5 am	0500	5 pm	1700
6 am	0600	6 pm	1800
7 am	0700	7 pm	1900
8 am	0800	8 pm	2000
9 am	0900	9 pm	2100
10 am	1000	10 pm	2200
11 am	1100	11 pm	2300

Playing Telephone

Dialing Instructions

Calling from Home (U.S.) to another Country. To dial direct, enter 011, then the country code, the city code (some countries do not require a city code because the country code applies everywhere), and the local telephone number. You can press the pound key "#" after this to save time on a touch-tone phone.

Sometimes you use a different number when calling inside a country than you use when calling from the United States—This is often the case when calling cell phones. The difference may be only an extra "0" in front of the local number but it can be confusing. If you can't reach someone and there is a "0" before the local number, try without the "0".

Example: You call 011 (international access code for US) 66 (Thailand country code) 2 (Bangkok city code) 07895647 (local number) and the call doesn't go through. Next, call without the "0" in front of the "7."

Calling from other Countries. Dial the international access code for the country you are calling from. When in doubt, try "00." Next dial the country code, the city code (note: some countries do not require a city code because the country code applies everywhere in the country), and then the local telephone number. You can also press the pound key "#" after this to save time on a touch-tone phone.

Typically, when you are calling the United States, you dial 001 and area code and the phone number.

It's not busy, it's just ringing!—the sounds of the dial tone and ring tones can be very different from what we are used to. Many U.S. people have hung up thinking a number was busy when the sound was the ring tone for that area.

Calling Home... Looking for Something Cheap and Easy

Buying a phone card in the United States—Not a good idea. Although you can purchase international calling cards in the United States to use abroad, the access codes are often difficult to use, the cards may have limited minutes, and can be expensive compared to getting one there.

Using your cell phone—maybe, but it's usually not cheap. In many places, you can use your U.S. cell phone, but the cost per minute may be very, very expensive. Your phone must be the right technology for the country's network—not every cell phone works in every country! Call your cell phone provider and find out if your phone will work where you are going and what the charges will be. Often, you need to activate the phone for service in the host country once you arrive, and your cell phone company will tell you how to do this. **Finally, you might go through all this and find out in country that the service doesn't work where you need it.**

Change to a global calling plan for your cell phone? You may be able to change your calling plan to a worldwide plan for when you are abroad and then change it back. Even with fees to make a change, this might be worth it to you.

Purchase an international calling card in the country you are visiting—The consistent winner! Typically this is the most cost-effective way to call home. Cards can often be bought at convenience stores, at tobacco shops, or close to travel hubs such as the airport or train station.

- **Get the right type of card!**—Some countries have different types—some can be used on payphones and land lines, others only on international payphones, some for local calls only, some international only.

- **Get some change, too. You might need change and the card to use a pay phone!**—when using a payphone in many countries, you must put in a small amount of change to call the access number for the calling card.

How to Use the Calling Code Chart

When calling from one country to another, use the country code in the third column. Some codes for major cities are listed under the country. When calling out of the country listed, use the International Access Code in the last column.

* These countries or islands are part of the North American numbering plan (similar to the United States)

** Dial the first number, wait for a second tone, and dial the second number.

International Calling Codes & Access Numbers

Country	Cities	Country Code	International Access Code
Afghanistan		93	00
Albania		355	00
	Durres	52	
	Tirana	42	
Algeria		213	00
	Adar	7	
	Algiers	2	
	Bejaia	5	
American Samoa		684	00
Andorra		376	00
Angola		244	00
	Luanda	2	
Argentina		54	00
	Buenos Aires	11	
	Cordoba	351	
	Rosario	41	
Armenia		374	
	Ashtarek	43	
	Yerevan	2	
Australia		54	0011
	Brisbane	7	
	Canberra	2	
	Melbourne	3	
	Sydney	2	
Australian Ex. Ter.		672	00
Austria		43	00
	Innsbruck	512	
	Vienna	1	
Azerbaijan		994	8~10**
Bahamas		1-242*	011

Country	Cities	Country Code	International Access Code
Bahrain		973	0
Bangladesh		880	00
	Chittagong	31	
	Dhaka (Dacca)	2	
	Khulna	41	
Barbados		1-246*	011
Belarus		375	8~10**
Belgium		32	00
	Antwerp	3	
	Brussels	2	
China		86	
Congo		242	00
Congo, Dem Rep		243	00
	Kinshasa	12	
Cook Island		682	00
Costa Rica		506	00
Cote d'Ivoire	(or Ivory Coast)	225	00
Croatia		385	00
	Dubrovnik	20	
	Zagreb	1	
Cuba		53	119
	Havana	7	
Cuba (Guant. Bay)		5399	00
Curacao		599	00
Cyprus		357	00
Czech Republic		420	00
	Prague	2	
Denmark		45	00
Diego Garcia		246	00
Djibouti		253	00
Dominica		1-767*	011
Dominican Rep.		1-809*	011
East Timor		670	00
Easter Island		56	00
Ecuador		593	00
	Guayaquil	4	
	Quito	2	
Egypt		20	00
	Alexandria	3	
	Cairo	2	
El Salvador		503	00
	El Paraiso	356	
	Los Lagartos	121	
Equatorial Guinea		240	00
Eritrea		291	00

Country	Cities	Country Code	International Access Code
	Asmara	1+	00
Estonia		372	8~10**
	Tallinn	6	
Ethiopia		251	00
	Addis Ababa	1	
	Awassa	6	
Fiji Islands		679	00
Finland		358	00
	Espoo	9	
	Helsinki	9	
France		33	00
French Antilles		596	00
French Guiana		594	00
French Polynesia	(or Tahiti)	689	00
Gabonese Rep.		241	00
Gambia		220	00
Georgia		995	8~10**
	Tblisi	3	
Germany		49	00
	Berlin	30	
	Frankfurt	69	
	Munich	89	
Ghana		233	00
	Accra	21	
	Kumasi	51	
Gibraltar		350	00
Greece		30	00
	Athens	210	
	Crete	2810	
	Sparta	731	
Greenland		299	
Grenada		1-473*	011
Guadeloupe		590	00
Guam		1-671*	011
Guatemala		502	00
Guinea-Bissau		245	00
Guinea		224	00
Guyana		592	001
	Georgetown	2	
Haiti		509	00
Honduras		504	00
Hong Kong		852	001
Hungary		36	00
	Budapest	1	
	Debrecen	52	

Country	Cities	Country Code	International Access Code
Iceland		354	00
India		91	00
	Bombay	22	
	Calcutta	33	
	New Delhi	11	
Indonesia		62	001,008
	Jakarta	21	
Iran		98	00
	Tabriz	41	
	Tehran	21	
Iraq		964	00
	Baghdad	1	
	Karbala	32	
Ireland		353	00
	Cork	21	
	Dublin	1	
Israel		972	00, 012, 013
	Jerusalem	2	
	Tel Aviv	3	
Italy		39	00
	Florence	055	
	Genoa	10	
	Milan	02	
	Naples	081	
	Rome	06	
	Venice	041	
	Vatican City	06	
Ivory Coast		225	00
Jamaica		1-876*	011
Japan		81	001, 0041
	Osaka	66	
	Tokyo	3	
	Yokohama	45	
Jordan		962	00
Kazakhstan		7	8~10**
Kenya		254	00
	Mombasa	11	
	Nairobi	20	
Kiribati		686	00
Korea (North)		850	00
Korea (South)		82	001, 002
	Kwangju	62	
	Pusan	51	
	Seoul	2	
	Taegu	53	

Country	Cities	Country Code	International Access Code
Kuwait		965	00
Kyrgyz Republic		996	00
Laos		856	14
	Vientiane	21	
Latvia		371	00
	Daugavpils	54	
Lebanon		961	00
	Beirut	1	
Lesotho		266	00
Liberia		231	00
Libya		218	00
	Benghazi	61	
	Tripoli	21	
Liechtenstein		423	00
Lithuania		370	8~10**
	Kaunas	37	
Luxembourg		352	00
Macao		853	00
Macedonia		389	00
	Skopje	2	
Madagascar		261	00
Malawi		265	00
Malaysia		60	00
	Kuala Lumpur	3	
Maldives		960	00
Mali Republic		223	00
Malta		356	00
Marshall Islands		692	011
Martinique		596	00
Mauritania		222	00
Mauritius		230	00
Mayotte Island		269	00
Mexico		52	00
	Acapulco	774	
	Cabo San Luc.	684	
	Cancun	98	
	Ensenada	617	
	Mazatlan	69	
	Mexicali	65	
	Mexico City	55	
	Puerto Vallarta	322	
	Tampico	121	
	Tijuana	6 or 66	
	Veracruz	29	
Micronesia		691	011

Country	Cities	Country Code	International Access Code
Midway Island		1-808*	011
Moldova		373	8~10**
Mongolia		976	00
	Ulan Bator	1	
Montserrat		1-664*	011
Morocco		212	00
	Casablanca	22	
	Rabat	37	
Mozambique		258	00
Myanmar		95	00
	Yangon	1	
Namibia		264	09
	Windhoek	61	
Nauru		674	00
Nepal		977	00
	Katmandu	1	
Netherlands		31	00
	Amsterdam	20	
	Rotterdam	10	
	The Hague	70	
Netherlands Ant.		599	00
	St. Maarten	5	
Nevis		1-869*	011
New Caledonia		687	00
New Zealand		64	00
	Auckland	9	
	Christ Church	3	
	Wellington	4	
Nicaragua		505	
	Leon	311	
	Managua	2	
Niger		227	00
Nigeria		234	009
	Lagos	1	
Niue Island		683	00
Norfolk Island		672	00
North Marianas Is.		1-670*	011
Norway		47	00
Oman		968	00
Pakistan		92	00
	Islamabad	51	
	Karachi	21	
Palau		680	011
Palestine		970	00
Panama		507	0

Country	Cities	Country Code	International Access Code
Papua New Guinea		675	05
Paraguay		595	00
	Asuncion	21	
	Concepcion	31	
Peru		51	00
	Lima	1	
Philippines		63	00
	Cebu City	32	
	Manila	2	
	Subic Bay	47	
Poland		48	0~0**
	Krakow	12	
	Warsaw	22	
	Manchester	161	
Portugal		351	00
	Lisbon	1	
Puerto Rico		1-787*	011
Qatar		974	00
Reunion Island		262	00
Romania		40	00
	Bucharest	1	
Russia		7	8~10**
	Moscow	095	
	St. Petersburg	812	
Rwanda		250	00
St. Helena		290	01
St. Kitts		1-869*	011
St. Lucia		1-758*	011
St. Pierre		508	00
St. Vincent	(Grenadines)	1-784*	011
Saipan		670	1
San Marino		378	00
Sao Tome	(Principe)	239	00
Saudi Arabia		966	00
Senegal		221	00
Serbia	(Montenegro)	381	99~00**
	Belgrade	11	
Seychelles		248	00
Sierra Leone		232	00
Singapore		65	001, 002
Slovakia		421	00
	Bratislava	2	
Slovenia		386	00
Solomon Is.		677	00
Somalia		252	19

Country	Cities	Country Code	International Access Code
South Africa		27	09
	Cape Town	21	
	Johannesburg	11	
	Pretoria	12	
Spain		34	00
	Barcelona	93	
	Madrid	91	
	Pamplona	948	
	Seville	95	
	Valencia	96	
Sri Lanka		94	00
	Columbo Cen.	1	
Sudan		249	00
Suriname		597	00
Swaziland		268	00
Sweden		46	00
	Stockholm	8	
Switzerland		268	00
	Berne	31	
	Geneva	22	
	Lausanne	21	
	Lucerne	41	
	Zurich	1	
Syria		963	00
	Damascus	11	
Taiwan		886	002
	Taipei	2	
Tajikistan		992	8~10**
Tanzania		255	000
	Dar Es Salaam	22	
	Tanga	27	
Thailand		66	001
	Bangkok	2	
	Chanthaburi	39	
Togo		228	00
Tokelau		690	00
Tonga Islands		676	00
Trinidad & Tobago		1-868*	011
Tunisia		216	00
	Bizerte	2	
	Tunis	1	
Turkey		90	00
	Ankara	312	
	Istanbul Avrupa	212	
	Istanbul Asya	216	

Country	Cities	Country Code	International Access Code
Turkmenistan		993	8~10**
Turks & Caicos Is.		1-649*	011
Tuvalu		688	00
Uganda		256	000
	Entebbe	42	
	Kampala	41	
Ukraine		380	8~10**
	Kiev	44	
	Odessa	482	
United Arab Emir.		971	00
	Abu Dhabi	2	
	Dubai	4	
United Kingdom		44	00
	Belfast	28	
	Glasgow	141	
	Liverpool	151	
	London	20	
United States		1	011
US Virgin Is.		1-340*	011
Uruguay		598	00
	Mercedes	532	
	Montevideo	2	
Uzbekistan		998	8~10**
Vanuatu		678	00
Vatican city		39	00
	All Points	6	
Venezuela		58	00
	Caracas	212	
	Maracaibo	61	
Vietnam		84	00
	Hanoi	4	
	Ho Chi Minh	8	
Wallis & Futuna		681	19
Western Samoa		685	00
Yemen		967	00
	Sana'a	1	
	Zabid	3	
Zambia		260	00
	Lusaka	1	
	Kitwe	2	
Zanzibar		255	00
Zimbabwe		263	00
	Bulawayo	9	
	Harare	4	

Airline Contact Information

Airline	Code	Toll-Free Phone	Out-of-Country Contact	Website
Aer Lingus	EI	1-800-223-6537	1-631-577-5700	www.aerlingus.com
Aero California	JR	1-800-237-6225	1-310-417-0004	www.aerocalifornia.de
Aeroflot	SU	1-888-340-6400	1-202-429-4922	www.aeroflot.com
Aerolineas Argentinas	AR	1-800-333-0276	1-212-542-8880	www.aeroargentinas.com
Aeromexico	AM	1-800-237-6639	None	www.aeromexico.com
Air Afrique	RK	None	+218 21 444 973 4	www.afriqiyah.aero
Air Algerie	AH	None	213 (0) 21 65 33 40 - 65 33 80/89 - 74 24 28	www.airalgerie.dz
Air Berlin	AB	None	+49 (30) 410 21 59 03	www.airberlin.com
Air Canada	AC	1-888-247-2262 1-800-268-0024 (group)	1-514-393-3333	www.aircanada.com
Air Europa	UX	1-800-238-7672	1-212-921-2381	www.air-europa.com
Air France	AF	1-800-237-2747	None	www.airfrance.com
Air India	AI	1-800-223-7776	1-212-407-1300	www.airindia.com
Air Jamaica	JM	1-800-523-5585	None	www.airjamaica.com
Air Malta	KM	None	0845 607 3710 U.K.	www.airmalta.com
Air Mauritius	MK	1-800-537-1182	1-201-871-8382	www.alrmauritius.com
Air Namibia	SW	1-800-626-4242	1-305-492-9049	www.airnamibia.com.na
Air Nauru	ON	None	1-310-670-7302	www.southpacific.org
Air New Zealand	NZ	1-800-262-1234	1-310-615-1111	www.airnz.com
Air Niugini (Papua New Guinea)	PX	0845 838 7901 U.K.	0870 240 2208 U.K.	www.airniugini.co.uk
Air Pacific (Fiji)	FJ	1-800-227-4446	1-310-568-8676	www.airpacific.com
Air Seychelles	HM	None	1-310-670-7302	www.airseychelles.net
Air Slovakia	GM	None	+44 121 55 5353 U.K.	www.airslovakia.sk
Air Srpska (Bosnia-Herzegovina)	R6	None	381 78 212 806 Bosnia	www.angelfire.com/biz3/Air Srpska/english.html
Air Sunshine	YI	1-800-327-8900		www.airsunshine.com
Air Transat	TS	1-877-872-6728		www.airtransat.ca
Air Tanzania	TC	None	0845 838 7901	www.airtanzania.com
Air Vanuatu	NF	1-800-677-4277	1-310-670-7302	www.pacificislands.com/airlines/vanuatu.html
AirTran Airways	FL	1-800-247-8726	1-770-994-8258	www.airtran.com
Alaska Airlines	AS	1-800-426-0333 1-800-445-4435 (group)	1-206-433-3200	www.alaskair.com
Alitalia	AZ	1-800-223-5730	None	www.alitalia.usa.com

Airline	Code	Toll-Free Phone	Out-of-Country Contact	Website
All Nippon Airways	NH	1-800 235-9262	1-310-782-3011	www.anaskyweb.com/us/e/
Aloha Airlines	AQ	1-800-367-5250	1-808-484-1111	www.alohaairlines.com
America West	HP	1-800-235-9292 1-800-428-4322	1-480-693-0800	www.americawest.com
American Airlines	AA	1-800-433-7300 1-800-221-2255 (group)	1-877-932-7322	www.aa.com
American Trans Air	TZ	1-800-225-2995	None	www.ata.com
Asiana Airlines	OZ	1-800-227-4262	1-213-365-4518	http://flyasiana.com/english
Austrian Airlines	OS	1-800-843-0002	1-718-670-8600	www.aua.com
Aviateca (Aerolineas de Guatemala)	GU	1-800-327-9832	None	www.aviateca.aero/
Bahamas Air	UP	1-800-222-4262	1-242-377-8454	www.bahamasair.com/online
Balkan Airlines	LZ	1-800-852-0944	None	www.balkan.com
Bemidji Airlines	CH	1-800-332-7133	1-218-751-1880 1-218-751-3726	www.bemidjiaviation.com/
British Airways	BA	1-800-247-9297	1-718-335-7070	www.britishairways.com
British Midland Airways (BMI)	BD	1-800-788-0555	None	www.flybmi.com
Cameroon Airlines	UY	1-800-677-4277	1-310-670-7302	www.cameroon-airlines.com
Cape Air	9K	1-800-352-0714	1-508-790-3122	http://www.flycapeair.com
Cathay Pacific Airlines	CX	1-800-233-2742	1-604-606-8888	www.cathay-usa.com
Cayman Airways	KX	1-800-422-9626	1-345-949-2311	www.caymanairways.com/
Cebu Pacific Air (Philippines)	5J	None	None	www.cebupacificair.com
China Airlines	CI	1-800-227-5118	None	www.china-airlines.com
China Eastern Airlines	MU	1-800-200-5118	None	www.chinaeastern.co.uk/
Continental	CO	1-800-525-0280 1-800-525-1700 (group)	1-281-821-2100	www.flycontinental.com
COPA	CM	1-800-359-2672	1-212-599-0882	www.copaair.com/
Czech Airlines	OK	1-800-223-2365	1-212-765-6545	www.czechairlines.com

Airline	Code	Toll-Free Phone	Out-of-Country Contact	Website
Cyprus Airways	CY	None	1-718-267-6882 NY	www.cyprusairways.com
Delta Airlines	DL	1-800-221-1212 1-800-337-4777 (group)	None	www.delta.com
Egypt Air	MS	1-800-334-6787	1-212-581-5600	www.egyptair.com.eg
El Al Israel	LY	1-800-223-6700	1-212-768-9200	www.elal.com
Emirates	EK	1-800-777-3999	None	www.emirates.com
Empire Airlines	EM	None	1-208-292-3850	www.empireairlines.com
Ethiopian Airlines	ET	1-800-445-2733	None	
Evergreen Airlines	0E	1-800-345-5556	1-503-472-0011	www.evergreenaviation.com
Finnair	AY	1-800-950-5000 1-800-950-4768	1-212-499-9000	www.finair.com
Frontier Airlines	F9	1-800-432-1359	1-907-474-0014	www.frontierairlines.com
Garuda Indonesia	GA	1-800-342-7832	0807-1-807807 Indonesia	www.garuda-Indonesia.com
Hawaiian Airlines	HA	1-800-367-5320	1-808-838-1555	www.hawaiianair.com
Horizon Air	QX	1-800-547-9308	1-206-241-6757	www.horizonair.com
Iberia Airlines of Spain	IB	1-800-772-4642 1-800-549-2770 (group)	None	www.iberia.com
Icelandair	FI	1-800-223-5500	None	www.icelandair.com
Japan Airlines	JL	1-800-525-3663 reserv 1-800-525-2355 info	None	www.japanair.com
JetBlue	B6	1-800-538-2583	1-801-365-2525	www.jetblue.com
Kenmore Air	5K	1-800-543-9595	1-425-486-1257	www.kenmoreair.com
Kenya Airways	KQ	1-866-536-9224	1-818-990-5923	www.kenya-airways.com
KLM Royal Dutch Airlines	KL	1-800-225-2525	1-671-649-8380	www.klm.nl
Korean Air	KE	1-800-438-5000	None	www.koreanair.com
Kuwait Airways	KU	1-800-621-2175	1-847-437-5455	www.kuwait-airways.com
Lan-Chile Airlines	LA	1-866-435-9526	None	www.lan.com
LanPeru	LP	1-866-435-9526	None	www.lan.com
Lloyd Aero Boliviano	LB	1-800-337-0918	1-305-374-4600	www.labairlines.com
Lot-Polish Airlines	LO	1-800-223-0593	1-212-789-0970	www.lot.com

Airline	Code	Toll-Free Phone	Out-of-Country Contact	Website
LTU International Airways	LT	1-800-888-0200	1-305-932-1595	www.ltu.com/world/
Lufthansa Airlines (German)	LH	1-800-645-3880	None	www.lufthansa-usa.com
Malaysia Airlines	MH	1-800-552-9264 reserv 1-800-233-5597 cargo	1-310-535-9288 1-310-215-4654 weekends/eves	www.malaysiaairlines.com
Malev Hungarian Airline	MA	1-800-223-6884	1-212-566-9944	www.malev.com
Mandarin Airlines	AE	None	(02) 2717 1230	www.mandarin-airlines.com
Martinair (Holland)	MP	1-800-627-8462	1-561-391-6165	www.martinairusa.com
Mexicana Airlines	MX	1-800-531-7921	1-305-599-4144	www.mexicana.com
Middle East Airlines	ME	None	1-310-338-9124 Los Angeles 1-212-244-6850 New York	www.mea.com.lb
Northwest Airlines/KLM	NW	1-800-225-2525 1-800-328-1111 (group)	1-612-726-2422 1-218-254-7725	www.nwa.com
Olympic Airlines	OA	1-800-223-1226	1-305-372-9500	www.olympicairlines.com
Pakistan International Airlines	PK	1-800-221-2552 1-800-578-6786 reserv	1-212-760-8142 1-212-971-9820	www.piac.com.pk
Pan American Airlines	PA	1-800-359-7262	1-603-766-2022	www.flypanam.com
Philippine Airlines	PR	1-800-435-9725	1-310-646-2411	www.philippineairlines.com
Polynesian Airlines	PH	1-800-264-0823	1-310-846-3181	www.polynesianairlines.com
Qantas Airways	QF	1-800-227-4500	1-718-995-2737	www.quantasusa.com
Reeve Aleutian Airways Inc.	RV	None	1-907-243-1112	www.alaskaair.com
Royal Air Maroc (Morocco)	AT	1-800-344-6726	1-212-750-6071	www.royalairmaroc.com
Royal Jordanian	RJ	1-800-223-0470	None	www.rja.com.jo
Ryan International Airlines	RY	1-800-727-0457	1-316-265-7400	www.flyryan.com

Airline	Code	Toll-Free Phone	Out-of-Country Contact	Website
Saudi Airlines	SV	1-800-472-8342	1-212-551-3020	www.saudiairlines.com
Scandinavian Airlines(SAS)	SK	1-800-221-2350	1-201-896-3735 fax	www.flysas.com
Singapore Airlines	SQ	1-800-742-3333	1-212-644-8801	www.singaporeair.com
Skywest	YT	1-800-453-9417	1-435-634-3000	www.skywest.com
Solomon Airlines	IE	1-800-677-4277	1-310-670-7302	www.solomonairlines.com.au
South African Airways	SA	1-800-722-9675 1-800-722-4768 (group)	1-954-769-5000	www.flysaa.com
Southwest Airlines	WN	1-800-435-9792 1-800-433-5368 (group)	1-214-792-4223	www.iflyswa.com www.southwest.com
Surinam Airways	PY	1-800-327-6864	1-305-599-1196	www.slm.firm.sr/nl
Swiss International Airlines	LX	1-877-359-7947	1-212-515-0319 fax	www.swiss.com
Syrian Arab Airlines		1-800-936-8300	None	www.syriaair.com
Taca	TA	1-800-535-8780	1-718-632-8222	www.taca.com
Tap Air Portugal	TP	1-800-221-7370	None	www.flytap.com
Tarom-Romanian Air Transport	RO	None	+40 21 2014768	www.tarom.ro/english
Thai Airways International	TG	1-800-426-5204	1-310-646-3090 1-662-628-2000	www.thaiair.com
Tropic Air (Belize)	CN	1-800-422-3435	None	www.tropicair.com
Turkish Airlines, Inc.	TK	1-800-874-8875	1-312-943-7858	www.turkishairlines.com
United Airlines	UA	1-800-864-8331 1-800-237-9524 (group)	1-800-538-2929	www.united.com
United Express	ZK	1-800-864-8331	None	www.united.com
US Airways	US	1-800-235-9292 1-800-428-4322	1-866-523-5333	www.usairways.com
Varig Brazilian Airlines	RG	1-800-468-2744	1-213-688-1900	www.varigbrasil.com
Virgin Atlantic Airways	VS	1-800-821-5438	None	www.virgin-atlantic.com
Yemenia Airways	IY	None	1-718-254-5867 NY	www.yemenia.com
Jat Airways (Yugoslavia)	JU	None	1-773-444-4050	www.jat.com
Air Zimbabwe	QZ	1-800-742-3006	1-818-501-2098 fax	www.airzimbabwe.com

Major International Airport Codes

Country	City	Airport Name	Airport Code
Algeria	Algiers	Houari Bourmedienne	ALG
Argentina	Buenos Aires	Ministro Pistarini	EZE
Australia	Adelaide	Adelaide	ADL
Australia	Brisbane	Brisbane Intl	BNE
Australia	Darwin	Darwin Intl	DRW
Australia	Melbourne	Melbourne	MEL
Australia	Perth	Perth Intl	PER
Australia	Sydney	Sydney Intl	SYD
Austria	Vienna	Vienna Intl	VIE
Belarus	Minsk	Minsk	MSQ
Belgium	Brussels	Brussels	BRU
Bolivia	La Paz	El Alto Intl	LPB
Bosnia-Herzegovina	Sarajevo	Sarajevo	SJJ
Brazil	Recife	Guararepes	REC
Brazil	Rio de Janeiro	Rio de Janeiro-Galeao Intl	GIG
Brazil	San Paulo	San Paulo-Guarulhos Intl	GRU
Bulgaria	Sofia	Sofia	SOF
Canada	Calgary	Calgary Intl	YYC
Canada	Edmonton	Edmonton Intl	YEG
Canada	Halifax	Halifax	YHZ
Canada	Montreal	Montreal-Dorval	YUL
Canada	Ottawa	Ottawa Intl	YOW
Canada	Toronto	Lester B Pearson Intl	YYZ
Canada	Vancouver	Vancouver Intl	YVR
Chile	Santiago	Arturo merino Benitez Intl	SCL
China	Beijing	Capital Intl	PEK
China	Hong Kong	Hong Kong Intl	HKG
China	Shanghai	Hong Qiao Intl	SHA
Columbia	Bogota	El Dorado Intl	BOG
Congo (Dem.Rep.of)	Kinshasa	Kinshasa N'Djili Intl	FIH
Costa Rica	San Jose	Juan Santamaria Intl	SJO
Croatia	Zagreb	Zagreb	ZAG

Country	City	Airport Name	Airport Code
Cuba	Havana	Jose Marti Intl	HAV
Czech Republic	Prague	Prague Ruzyne	PRG
Denmark	Copenhagen	Copenhagen	CPH
Dominican Republic	Santo Domingo	Las Americas	SDQ
Ecuador	Quito	Mariscal Sucre Intl	UIO
Egypt	Cairo	Cairo Intl	CAI
El Salvador	San Salvador	Comalapa Intl	SAL
Estonia	Tallinn	Tallinn Yulemiste	TLL
Ethiopia	Addis Ababa	Bole Intl	ADD
Finland	Helsinki	Helsinki-Vantaa	HEL
France	Bordeaux	Bordeaux	BOD
France	Marseille	Marseille Provence	MRS
France	Nice	Nice Cote d'Azur	NCE
France	Paris	Paris Charles de Gaulle	CDG
France	Paris	Le Bourget	LBG
France	Paris	Paris Orly	PRY
Germany	Berlin	Tegel	TXL
Germany	Berlin	Tempelhof	THF
Germany	Cologne	Cologne-Bonn	CGN
Germany	Dusseldorf	Dusseldorf Intl	DUS
Germany	Frankfurt	Frankfurt Main	FRA
Germany	Hamburg	Hamburg Intl	HAM
Germany	Munich	Munchen Intl	MUC
Germany	Stuttgart	Stuttgart	STR
Greece	Athens	Eleftherios Venizelos	ATH
Guatemala	Guatemala City	La Aurora	GUA
Haiti	Port-au-Prince	Mais Gate	PAP
Honduras	Tegucigalpa	Toncontin	TGU
Hungary	Budapest	Budapest Ferihegy	BUD
Iceland	Keflavik	Keflavik Intl	KEF
India	Calcutta	Calcutta Intl	CCU
India	Mumbai (Bombay)	Chhatrapari Shivaji Intl	BOM
India	New Delhi	Indira Ghandi Intl	DEL
Indonesia	Jakarta	Halim Perdana Kusuma	HLP
Indonesia	Jakarta	Soekamo-Hatta Jakarta	CGK

Country	City	Airport Name	Airport Code
Iran	Tehran	Mehrabad Intl	THR
Iraq	Baghdad	Baghdad Intl	BGW
Ireland	Dublin	Dublin	DUB
Ireland	Shannon	Shannon	SNN
Israel	Tel Aviv	Ben Gurion Intl	TLV
Italy	Bologna	Bologna G. Marconi Intl	BLQ
Italy	Milan	Milan Linate Intl	LIN
Italy	Milan	Milan Malpensa Intercontinent	MXP
Italy	Naples	Naples Intl	NAP
Italy	Pisa	Pisa Galileo Galilei	PSA
Italy	Rome	Rome Leonardo da Vinci-Fiumicino	FCO
Italy	Venice	Venice Marco Polo	VCE
Japan	Osaka	Kansai Intl	KIX
Japan	Tokyo	Tokyo Haneda Intl	HND
Japan	Tokyo	New Tokyo Intl	NRT
Jordan	Amman	Wueen Alia Intl	AMM
Kenya	Nairobi	Jomo Kenyatta Intl	NBO
Kuwait	Kuwait City	Kuwait Intl	KWI
Lebanon	Beirut	Beirut Intl	BEY
Lithuania	Vilnius	Vilnius	VNO
Malaysia	Kuala Lampur	Kuala Lampur Intl	KUL
Mexico	Mexico City	Licenciado Benito Juarez	MEX
Morocco	Casablanca	Mohammad V	CMN
Myanmar (Burma)	Yangon	Yangon Intl	RGN
Nepal	Katmandu	Tribhuvan Intl	KTM
Netherlands	Amsterdam	Schiphol	AMS
New Zealand	Auckland	Auckland Intl	AKL
Nicaragua	Managua	Augusto Sandino	MGA
Norway	Oslo	Oslo	OSL
Pakistan	Islamabad	Islamabad Intl	ISB
Panama	Panama City	Tocumen Intl	PTY
Papua New Guinea	Port Moresby	Port Moresby Jacksons Intl	POM
Paraguay	Asuncion	Silvio Pettriossi	ASU

Country	City	Airport Name	Airport Code
Peru	Lima	Jorge Chavez Lima-Callao Intl	LIM
Philippines	Manila	Ninoy Aquino Intl	MNL
Poland	Warsaw	Warsaw Frederic Chopin	WAW
Portugal	Lisbon	Lisboa	LIS
Romania	Bucharest	Otepeni	OTP
Russia	Moscow	Sheremetyevo Intl	SVO
Russia	Moscow	Vnukovo	VKO
Russia	St. Petersburg	Pulkovo	LED
Saudi Arabia	Jeddah	King Abdulaziz Intl	JED
Senegal	Dakar	Yoff	DKR
Singapore	Singapore	Singapore Changi	SIN
South Africa	Cape Town	Cape Town Intl	CPT
South Africa	Johannesburg	Johannesburg Intl	JNB
South Korea	Seoul	Kimpo Intl	SEL
Spain	Madrid	Madrid Barajas	MAD
Sri Lanka	Colombo	Katunayake	CMB
Sudan	Khartoum	Khartoum	KRT
Sweden	Stockholm	Stockholm Arlanda	ARN
Switzerland	Geneva	Geneva Intl	GVA
Switzerland	Zurich	Zurich	ZRH
Syrian Arab Republic	Damascus	Damascus Intl	DAM
Taiwan	Taipei	Chiang Kai Shek Intl	TPE
Thailand	Bangkok	Bangkok Intl	BKK
Tunisia	Tunis	Carthage	TUN
Turkey	Istanbul	Ataturk Intl	IST
Uganda	Kampala	Entebbe	EBB
Ukraine	Kiev	Borispol	KBP
U.K. England	Birmingham	Birmingham Intl	BHX
U.K. England	London	Gatwick	LGW
U.K. England	London	Heathrow	LHR
U.K. England	London	London City	LCY
U.K. England	London	London Stansted	STN
U.K. England	London	London Luton	LTN
U.K. England	Manchester	Manchester	MAN

Country	City	Airport Name	Airport Code
U.K. N.Ireland	Belfast	Belfast City	BHD
U.K. Scotland	Edinburgh	Edinburgh	EDI
U.K. Scotland	Glasgow	Glasgow	GLA
United Arab Emirates	Abu Dhabi	Abu Dhabi Intl	AUH
Uruguay	Montevideo	Carrasco	MVD
U.S. Territory	Guam Island	Guam Intl	GUM
Venezuela	Caracas	Simon Bolivar Intl	CCS
Vietnam	Ho Chi Mihn City	Tan Son Nhut Intl	SGN
Yugoslavia	Belgrade	Belgrade	BEG

Air Freight Companies

Airborne Express	800-426-2323
DHL Courier Express	800-225-5345
Emery Worldwide	800-443-6379
Federal Express	800-238-5355
UPS	800-742-5877

Rental Car Agencies, Driving Insurance, & Other Info

Rental Car Agency	Toll-Free Phone Numbers	Out-of-Country Contact Numbers
Advantage	1-800-777-5500 Reservations 1-800-777-5524 Customer Service	210-247-2869
Alamo	1-800-327-9633	801-533-4441
Avis	1-800-352-7900	757-687-2000
Budget	1-800-527-0700	509-838-8662 (Spokane Intl, WA)
Dollar	1-800-800-4000	918-665-3930
Enterprise	1-800-325-8007	314-427-7757 (St. Louis Airport, MO)
Hertz	1-800-654-3001	405-681-2341 (Will Rodgers Airport, OK)
National	1-800-227-3876	801-575-2277 (Salt Lake City Airport, UT)
Payless Car Rental	1-800-729-5377	727-321-6352
Thrifty	1-800-847-4389	918-665-3930

International Driver's License. Even though it does not require much to obtain, authorities in many host countries treat this as much more than just another document, so it can be worth getting. The requirements really only involve a driver's license. In essence, having this provides what's on your driver's license in several different languages but not anything more. The license may be picked up at any AAA location, $10 cost (in 2005).

Insurance.

Before driving in other countries, verify with your auto insurance that you are insured when driving a rental car outside the United States and what coverage that includes. Even if you are covered, it may be a good idea in some countries, such as Mexico, to pay for the additional insurance offered by the rental agency. When Mexican authorities sort out liability for an accident, for example, having rental car coverage from the Mexican car agency has made a difference in being detained.

Some credit card companies provide accident, loss or damage coverage for rental cars, called collision damage waiver (CDW). In the United States, many people decline the insurance that a rental agency offers because it is expensive for what it provides and usually duplicates a person's credit card coverage. This may not be the best decision outside the United States. See the note above for Mexico. If you decide to decline the insurance, make sure your decision is clear on the form, so as to not get charged.

Roadside Assistance Info. When making a reservation, get the direct phone number for "Roadside Assistance." To get the right phone number, tell them the country you will be calling from.

Contacting the U.S. Offices. When calling from other countries, remember that most of the numbers are within the United States, on the corresponding local U.S. time.

Keep Records of any rental car agent you speak to when reporting any problems with the car. Keep track of any paperwork or phone numbers.

Credit Card Holds. The rental agency may put a hold on the credit card for a specified amount, which means that your credit card limit will be decreased by that amount.

Inspecting a Rental Vehicle. Be sure to give a rental vehicle a close inspection and note any damage on a form provided. If you want, take digital pictures of the specific damaged areas to document how you are receiving the vehicle, but you need to include in the photo a legible view of the document you are submitting to verify the date you are taking the photos.

Have an Accident Plan. Research what happens in your host country after an accident and plan what you would do, for example, what the authorities typically do, whom you should call, what you should or shouldn't say, and so on.

Credit Card Contact Information & Fee Warnings

If your credit cards are stolen, it can help to have a list of your credit card numbers that you keep separate from your wallet or purse. Tip: Make more than one copy and leave one in each of your bags. If your credit card is stolen, most likely you are not responsible for more than $50 in fraudulent charges.

	US Number	World Number
MasterCard	800-622-7747	636-722-7111
Visa Worldwide	800-847-2911	410-581-9994
Discover Card	800-347-2683	801-902-3100
American Express	800-528-4800	336-393-1111
Diners Club Int./Carte Blanche	800-288-6378	303-799-1504

Most credit card companies will convert the currency from the foreign country's currency to U.S. dollars on your next statement. Many times they charge a fee for the conversion.

Find out about your card's international fees! When getting cash withdrawals using a credit card you may get a better exchange rate but will typically be charged service fees and maybe a foreign country charge fee, and maybe cash advance fees and maybe a currency conversion fee. If you can, find out what these fees are (some fees are hard to know about until they show up on your statement, too late to avoid).

New fees are appearing for international transactions! Even if you traveled in the last few years and didn't have these kinds of fees when using your credit card, you may want to check if the card's fees have changed. The trend the last few years has been for cards to add new fees for foreign country charges. While it looked as if traveler's checks were becoming obsolete in favor of credit cards, these new fees could change what is the best balance of safety and cost.

Tip: You may be able to avoid cash withdrawal fees by *overpaying* your credit card before you leave, so you have a credit card balance (this is a great trick that has worked—but there is no guarantee how your card handles this).

Non-U.S. Electrical Info
Voltage

The voltage of the electricity in another country can be different—a member of your group may plug the hair dryer brought from home into an outlet and get a nasty electrical surge and a ruined hair dryer. In the U.S. we use 110volts/60Hz and the appliances we buy are set for that voltage. Most countries use 220volts/50Hz. A voltage converter or a transformer lets you plug your U.S. devices into outlets in a country that uses different voltage. First, determine what the voltage is in the host country.

Transformers vary by what kind of wattage they deliver. Check the wattage of the item or items that you are going to be using (don't forget the service equipment you will be bringing) and get the appropriate transformer. Typical transformer types are as follows:

- 0 to 50 watts. These are typically used for tasks such as charging batteries where a low constant electricity level is needed.

- 50 to 2000 watts. These are used for appliances or items that need much more power (e.g., a hairdryer)

- Both (0 to 2000). These transformers are ideal because they can be used for both situations. They may cost a bit more, but you will have the capability of using it for something unexpected.

Tip: Many electronic devices, such as laptop computers, are being made to be compatible from 110 to 220, but not all, so be careful and check the specs for your model before risking frying it by plugging it in.

Plugs (what you plug your electrical devices into)

The plugs in other countries can vary from ours as much as our wildflowers vary from theirs. Luckily, you just put an adapter on your device's or transformer's plug to have your device work. The following lists some plugs and their "natural habitats." Adapter kits are widely available. The trick is having the right one, and for service projects, having the right number of adapters.

International Electrical Plugs

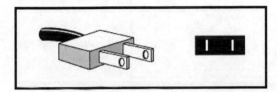

Plug A is ungrounded, used mostly in North America, Japan, South America, and much of the Caribbean Islands.

Plug B is a grounded plug used in North and South America, Japan and much of the Caribbean Islands.

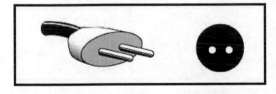

Plug C is called the Europlug and is used in Africa, the Middle East, Asia, and Europe. It is one of the most common plugs in the world.

Plug D is used in India, Africa, and some parts of the Middle East.

Plug E is used in France, Belgium, Czech Republic, Poland, and some parts of Africa.

Plug F is called the Schuko Plug and is used in Germany, Greece, Hungary, Scandinavia, Portugal, Romania, and Spain.

Plug G is used in the UK, Ireland, and present/ former UK colonies, Africa, India, Asia, and Middle East.

Plug H is ungrounded, used in Argentina China, Australia, New Zealand, & throughout the South Pacific.

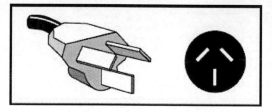

Plug J is grounded, used in Argentina, China, Australia, New Zealand, & throughout the South Pacific.

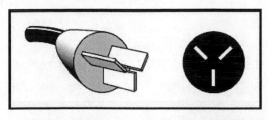

Plug K is unique to Israel

Plug L is used in Denmark and some in Africa.

Plug M is used in Switzerland.

Plug N is used in Italy, Ethiopia, and most of Chile.

Plug P is used in South Africa, and India.

Plug Q is used in Russia (similar to Plug C but the pins are only 4 mm).

Video & Audio

Television Standards

There are five: NTSC, SECAM, PAL, N-PAL, and M-PAL. Each operates on different frequencies and they are not compatible with each other. Keep this in mind if you are bringing broadcast or similar equipment.

DVDs and Regional Codes

If you are planning to show DVDs, you may run into some problems with regional codes. You avoid these if you are playing a DVD you bought in the U.S. on your laptop computer or on equipment you brought from the U.S. In other cases, read the following to avoid some frustration.

Most DVDs of movies and copyrighted material have been encoded so they cannot play in regions other than where they were purchased. This is done mainly because when a video is released in certain countries it hasn't come out in theaters in other countries. The movie makers do not want you to be able to watch a movie at home that is playing in the theater.

In addition to encoding, most discs manufactured in certain regions will play only on players manufactured in the same region. Discs without any coding can be played in any region, and on any player (this applies to DVDs you might make yourself, for instance, video you took yourself—homemade DVDs of non-copyrighted material should be OK). The regional info is usually on the back of the DVD package, either stating a region, or "Available Worldwide." Also, there is often a "globe logo" with the region number, or the word "ALL". There are six regions as follows:

- Region 1: U.S., U.S. Territories, and Canada
- Region 2: Europe, Japan, the Middle East (including Egypt) South Africa, and Greenland
- Region 3: Southeast Asia, East Asia (including Hong Kong but not China)

- Region 4: Mexico, South America, Central America, Australia, New Zealand, Pacific Islands, and the Caribbean

- Region 5: Former Soviet Union, Eastern Europe, India, North Korea, Mongolia, and most of Africa

- Region 6: China (excluding Hong Kong)

Also, if you are planning on showing VHS, confirm that the equipment you are planning on using matches the media you are using. There are different sizes of videocassettes and formats.

Video, Audio, and Computer Cables and Connections

You may want to hook up your computer to a host country person's printer or connect your VCR to their television. The following section goes over the connections and cables that short-term mission groups commonly need. Each of the following cables has different types of connections of each end, called a male type of connection and a female type of connection. These should match up to what you are planning to connect the ends to. For instance, a female connection cannot attach to another female connection.

 **USB (Universal Serial Bus) Connections** connect various things to a computer, whether PCs or Macs. They connect mice, printers, keyboards, "flash drives" (portable storage), iPods, and other portable music devices. There are two types of USB connectors. Type A is the most common and usually hooked up to the computer, while type B is used for things such as digital cameras or to hook to a printer. There are two different types of USB based on speed: USB 1 and USB 2. Both will work but USB 2 will be faster if the devices are USB 2 devices, so you may have faster equipment if you bring only USB 2 cables. Some USB cables are

especially designed to connect only to certain equipment. For instance, there may be a standard USB connection that plugs into a computer's USB port on one end of the cable but the other end is designed only to connect into a Canon camera or a Motorola cell phone or a Sony video camera. Usually these specialized USB cables come with the equipment they work with.

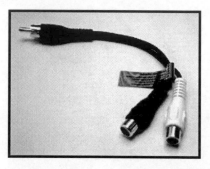

RCA cables (composite cables) connect VCRs, DVD players, or stereo equipment to each other or to TVs. They are often color-coded: yellow for video, white for left audio, and red for right audio. The picture shows an RCA cable to connect an audio in or out source to a right speaker in or out source (red) and left speaker in or out source (white). The yellow video RCA cable isn't shown.

Component Cables are like RCA composite cables, except that the video is split into three cables, instead of using just one. This allows better video quality. The colors usually match to what they are being plugged into.

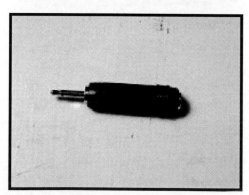

1/8" Audio Plug. This plug is often used with portable electronics such as headphones, small speakers, and CD players.

1/4" Audio Plug. This plug provides a better connection,

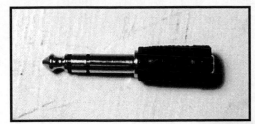

typically with musical instruments or equipment, such as guitars, keyboards, amplifiers, or mixing boards.

XLR. This audio plug is typically used to connect vocal microphones to amplifiers or mixers.

Tip: There are different connectors that can be used to connect 1/8", 1/4", XLR, and RCA cables, so you can use them interchangeably but carefully think through what cable is going where so you can get the appropriate ends (either male or female).

Conversions & Measures

Most of the world measures things using the metric system. The handy comparisons in the following tables can help you work with your group members to understand what amounts you and your host ministry partners are working with.

Weights

1 kilogram =	2.2 pounds
30 grams =	about 1 ounce (1.06 oz.)

Liquid Measure

1 liter =	about 1 quart (1.06 quarts) 1 gallon = 4 quarts
500 milliliters =	about 1 pint (1.06 pints) 1 quart = 2 pints
30 milliliters =	about 1 fluid ounce (1.01 oz.)

Lengths

1 kilometer =	0.62 miles	3281 feet	1094 yards
1 meter =	1.0936 yards	3 feet, 3 1/3 inches	
30 centimeters =	about 1 foot (30.5 centimeters)		
1 centimeter =	0.3937 inches		

Area

1 square kilometer	= 247 acres
1 square meter =	1.196 square yards 10.76 square foot 1,550 square inches

Volume

1 cubic meter =	1.3 cubic yard 35.3 cubic foot
1 cubic centimeter =	0.061 cubic inches

Temperature

Fahrenheit to Celsius formula... Celsius= 5/9 x (Fahrenheit – 32)

Celsius to Fahrenheit formula... Fahrenheit= 9/5 x Celsius + 32

"Real-World Situations" Temperature Reference	Fahrenheit (degrees)	Celsius (degrees)
Freezing point of water	32	0
Wear a sweater	50	10
Comfortable in a T-shirt or short sleeves	70	21
Hot – drink enough water	95	35
Very hot – drink before getting thirsty to keep hydrated	105	40
At the limits of safety for outside weather	110	43
Boiling point of water	212	100
Typical oven temperature	350	175

Driving Speeds — Handy Conversions

Kilometers per hour	Miles per hour
25	16
60	37
80	50
100	62
130	81

Construction

The following section can help both the experienced construction person and the inexperienced. A resource for both, it can also help the experienced person make explanations (showing what's needed when language or experience barriers exist) or delegate tasks, such as purchasing supplies.

Saw Blades

The **40 Tooth Blade** is used for a smoother cut, it requires less power and less material waste

The **20 Tooth Blade** is used for construction grade material.

The **Vinyl and Paneling Blade** uses fine teeth to make it easier to cut thin materials.

Screws

Pan Head has a flatter surface under the head, and gives you more power when attaching things.

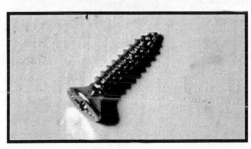

Flat Head is most commonly used when a flat surface is required. It can be flush with the surface, or driven in further and have a plug covering the screw head.

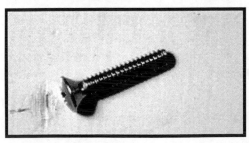

Round Head is designed like it has a built in washer. It can handle and disperse more stress than other screws, due to this feature.

Oval Head is used when you need a more finished look. The head sits just on top of the surface, and is smooth so it doesn't snag.

Nails

You'll want to make sure you use the right length nail and the right type of nail for what you are doing. The types will be the same in the country you visit. The way lengths are described will be a little different.

- In the United States, nails are categorized by their size in pennies (the symbol used is d). The rest of the world describes nails by length and diameter and uses millimeters (mm). Your host country partner will look at you funny if you ask for a 10 penny nail.

- A 6d finishing nail and a 6d common nail are the same length but have different diameters or gauges.

- The formula is roughly $(1/2)+(1/4)n$ inches long for an n-penny nail. When the size of nail goes up one unit in pennies it goes up a quarter of an inch in length. For example a 2d nail is 1 inch long, and a 3d nail is 1 1/4 inches long.

If you are unsure what length nail to use, a good rule is that a nail's length should be three times the thickness of the board that it is going through to fasten that board securely to another board or other object.

Types of Nails

Common Nails- used for general construction purposes. The nail heads are visible when they have been driven

Box Nails- used in lighter construction their shanks and heads are slightly narrower than common nails

Finishing Nails—much smaller head, normally used when appearance matters or when nailing trim.

Roofing Nails—larger head than most nails, used to hold shingles and usually are galvanized

Drywall Nails—used with drywall, same as roofing nails, but not galvanized

Lumber

Hardwood. Many hardwoods are not "hard" but softer than some woods that aren't called hardwood. The name hardwood means lumber from a tree that has a broad leaf is normally deciduous trees (those that shed leaves in the fall).

Hardwoods are measured by 1/4 inch units of thickness. A 4/4 is 1 inch, 6/4 is 1 1/2 inches, and so forth.

Softwood. Lumber from trees with needled leafs, usually coniferous evergreens (trees that are green all year round).

Softwoods are graded for specific uses. There are many grades, and classes. For example, for light framing you should use lumber 2–4 inches and 4 inches wide. For structural light framing, you should use lumber 2–4 inches thick and 2–4 inches wide, the same dimensions go for studs and appearance framing. For structural joists and planks, the lumber should be 2–4 inches wide, and 6 inches or wider.

Plywood. Plywood comes in sheets of 4'-0" wide and 8'-0" long and thicknesses of 1/8", 1/4", 3/8", 1/2", 5/8", and 3/4."

Lumber Sizing

Lumber called 2x4 has an actual size of 1 1/2 x 3 1/2. The following chart shows other sizes. The nominal size is the size of the lumber before it has been treated. The actual size is the minimum acceptable size after it has been treated. When discussing specific pieces of lumber, use the nominal size. This is the most common term that you will find used in a lumber yard. Also included in the chart are the metric conversions.

Lumber — Handy Conversions

Nominal	Actual	Actual Metric
1 x 2	3/4 x 1 1/2	19 x 38 mm
1 x 3	3/4 x 2 1/2	19 x 64mm
1 x 4	3/4 x 3 1/2	19 x 89mm
1 x 5	3/4 x 4 1/2	19 x 114mm
1 x 6	3/4 x 5 1/2	19 x 140mm
1 x 8	3/4 x 7 1/2	19 x 184mm
1 x 10	3/4 x 9 1/2	19 x 235mm
1 x 12	3/4 x 11 1/2	19 x 286mm
1 1/4 x 4	1 x 3 1/2	25 x 89mm
1 1/4 x 6	1 x 5 1/2	25 x 140mm
1 1/4 x 8	1 x 7 1/4	25 x 184mm
1 1/4 x 10	1 x 9 1/4	25 x 235mm
1 1/4 x 12	1 x 11 1/4	25 x 286mm
1 1/2 x 4	1 1/4 x 3 1/2	32 x 89mm
1 1/2 x 6	1 1/4 x 5 1/2	32 x 140mm
1 1/2 x 8	1 1/4 x 7 1/4	32 x 184mm
1 1/2 x 10	1 1/4 x 9 1/4	32 x 235mm
1 1/2 x 12	1 1/4 x11 1/4	32 x 286mm
2 x 4	1 1/2 x 3 1/2	38 x 89mm
2 x 6	1 1/2 x 5 1/2	38 x 140mm
2 x 8	1 1/2 x 7 1/4	38 x 184mm
2 x 10	1 1/2 x 9 1/4	38 x 235mm
2 x 12	1 1/2 x11 1/4	38 x 286mm
3 x 6	2 1/2 x 5 1/2	64 x 140mm
4 x 4	3 1/2 x 3 1/2	89 x 89mm
4 x 6	3 1/2 x 5 1/2	89 x 140mm

Concrete

Concrete is made of mixed cement, sand, and gravel (or course aggregate). When you add water, the ingredients bind into a solid. A basic mix for concrete is 1 part cement, 2 parts sand, and 3 parts gravel or other course aggregate. The "recipe" affects the strength and other attributes of the finished concrete. Different projects call for different mixes. Here are some practical uses, and their mixtures.

Basic Concrete Mixtures

Cement:Sand:Gravel Ratio	Uses
1:2.5:5	Normal foundations and walls
1:2.5:3	Floors (light duty), driveways
1:2.25:3	Steps, sidewalks
1:2:4	Reinforced roads, buildings, walls
1:1:1.5	Fence posts

Recipe

Mix sand and cement first until it is all the same color

Add the aggregate or gravel.

Add water. Be careful that you don't add too much or the mix will become too watery. Too little water will make the mix too hard to work with. Add enough to make the mixture workable. The less water you add, the stronger your concrete will be.

Rectangle and Circle Formulas

Area is the number of square units needed to measure a figure.

Circle

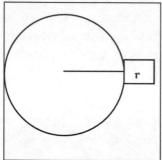

Area = πr2 (pi times r(radius) squared)

Circumference = 2πr (2times pi times r)
r = radius
π = pi (approximately 3.14)

Rectangle

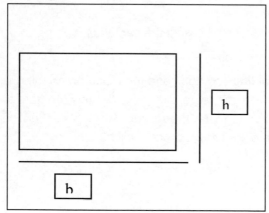

Area = b x h (base times height)

b = base   h = height

Need to Tie a Good Knot?

When you are in the field, you may need to tie something down. Knowing how to tie the right knot for the job can save you time, and potentially save your luggage from tumbling in the mud.

> Tip: Determine which knot is right for each end of the rope. Some knots tighten under load, some need a load to stay tight, some are easier to untie after a load has been put on them than other knots are.

Some Potential Situations & a Good Knot to Use

Situation	A good knot for this is a...
Tying down a tarp that has rope-holes on a loaded vehicle	Lark's Head

Situation	A good knot for this is a...
For tying fishing line to hooks or flies	Improved Clinch Knot

Situation	A good knot for this is a...
Need something at end of a lifeline or at the end of a rope to stop it from going through a block	Flemish Knot (also called Figure-8)

Situation	A good knot for this is a...
For shortening the length of a rope	Sheep Shank

Situation	A good knot for this is a...
Tying down luggage or something like a canoe on top of a van	Trucker's Hitch

Situation	A good knot for this is a...
Fastening a rope to a post	Rolling Hitch (Magnus Hitch)

Situation	A good knot for this is a...
Tying a boat to a dock	Double Half Hitch and The Round Turn

Situation	A good knot for this is a...
Rescuing someone with a rope around their waist or chest (under the arms) Or for safely tying around the neck of a stock animal	Bowline

Situation	A good knot for this is a...
Securing a tent-rope to a stake, allows adjustment of tension	Tautline Hitch

Situation	A good knot for this is a...
For towing or hauling something this knot won't slip	Timber Hitch

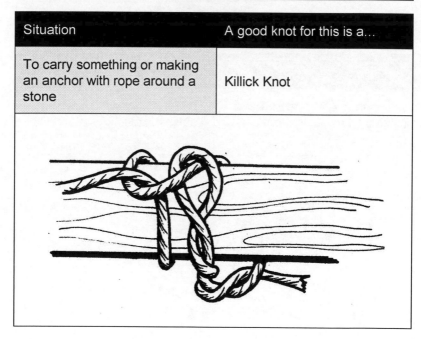

Situation	A good knot for this is a...
To carry something or making an anchor with rope around a stone	Killick Knot

Situation	A good knot for this is a...
For tying up a stock animal to a post	Constrictor Hitch for connecting to the post (Use a bowline around the animal's neck)

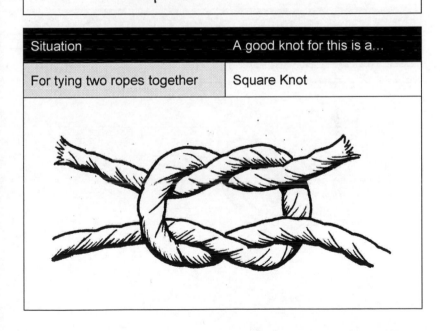

Situation	A good knot for this is a...
For tying two ropes together	Square Knot

Situation	A good knot for this is a...
Fast way to secure a rope to a hook	Blackwell Hitch Knot

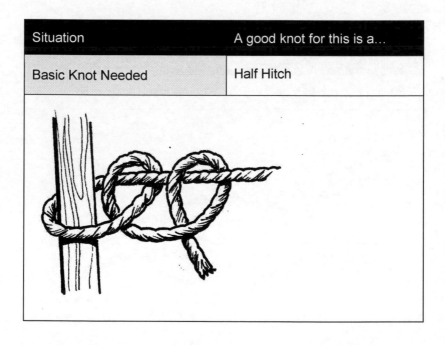

Situation	A good knot for this is a...
Basic Knot Needed	Half Hitch

Clothing Sizes

Men's

Suits

American	European	UK
32	42	32
34	44	34
36	46	36
38	48	38
40	50	40
42	52	42
44	54	44
46	56	46

Shirts

American	European	UK
14	36	14
14 1/2	37	14 1/2
15	38	15
15 1/2	39	15 1/2
16	40	16
16 1/2	41	16 1/2
17	42	17
17 1/2	43	17 1/2

Shoes

American	European	UK
7	40	6 1/2
7 1/2	40-41	7
8	41	7 1/2
8 1/2	41-42	8
9	42-43	8 1/2
9 1/2	43	9
10	43-44	9 1/2
10 1/2	44	10
11	45	10 1/2
11 1/2	45-46	11
12	46	11 1/2

Women's

Dresses /Suits/Pants/Sweaters

American	European	UK
6	36	8
8	38	10
10	40	12
12	42	14
14	44	16
16	46	18
18	48	20
20	50	22
22	52	24

Shoes

American	European	UK
5	36-37	3 1/2
5 1/2	37	4
6	37-38	4 1/2
6 1/2	38	5
7	38-39	5 1/2
7 1/2	39	6
8	39-40	6 1./2
8 1/2	40	7
9	40-41	7 1/2
9 1/2	41	8
10	41-42	8 1/2
10 1/2	42	9
11	42-43	9 1/2

Calendars

The following pages provide calendars for 2006 through 2011.

January

s	m	t	w	t	f	s
1	2	3	4	5	6	7
8	9	10	11	12	13	14
15	16	17	18	19	20	21
22	23	24	25	26	27	28
29	30	31				

February

s	m	t	w	t	f	s
			1	2	3	4
5	6	7	8	9	10	11
12	13	14	15	16	17	18
19	20	21	22	23	24	25
26	27	28				

March

s	m	t	w	t	f	s
			1	2	3	4
5	6	7	8	9	10	11
12	13	14	15	16	17	18
19	20	21	22	23	24	25
26	27	28	29	30	31	

April

s	m	t	w	t	f	s
						1
2	3	4	5	6	7	8
9	10	11	12	13	14	15
16	17	18	19	20	21	22
23	24	25	26	27	28	29
30						

May

s	m	t	w	t	f	s
	1	2	3	4	5	6
7	8	9	10	11	12	13
14	15	16	17	18	19	20
21	22	23	24	25	26	27
28	29	30	31			

June

s	m	t	w	t	f	s
				1	2	3
4	5	6	7	8	9	10
11	12	13	14	15	16	17
18	19	20	21	22	23	24
25	26	27	28	29	30	

July

s	m	t	w	t	f	s
						1
2	3	4	5	6	7	8
9	10	11	12	13	14	15
16	17	18	19	20	21	22
23	24	25	26	27	28	29
30	31					

August

s	m	t	w	t	f	s
		1	2	3	4	5
6	7	8	9	10	11	12
13	14	15	16	17	18	19
20	21	22	23	24	25	26
27	28	29	30	31		

September

s	m	t	w	t	f	s
					1	2
3	4	5	6	7	8	9
10	11	12	13	14	15	16
17	18	19	20	21	22	23
24	25	26	27	28	29	30

October

s	m	t	w	t	f	s
1	2	3	4	5	6	7
8	9	10	11	12	13	14
15	16	17	18	19	20	21
22	23	24	25	26	27	28
29	30	31				

November

s	m	t	w	t	f	s
			1	2	3	4
5	6	7	8	9	10	11
12	13	14	15	16	17	18
19	20	21	22	23	24	25
26	27	28	29	30		

December

s	m	t	w	t	f	s
					1	2
3	4	5	6	7	8	9
10	11	12	13	14	15	16
17	18	19	20	21	22	23
24	25	26	27	28	29	30
31						

January

s	m	t	w	t	f	s
	1	2	3	4	5	6
7	8	9	10	11	12	13
14	15	16	17	18	19	20
21	22	23	24	25	26	27
28	29	30	31			

February

s	m	t	w	t	f	s
				1	2	3
4	5	6	7	8	9	10
11	12	13	14	15	16	17
18	19	20	21	22	23	24
25	26	27	28			

March

s	m	t	w	t	f	s
				1	2	3
4	5	6	7	8	9	10
11	12	13	14	15	16	17
18	19	20	21	22	23	24
25	26	27	28	29	30	31

April

s	m	t	w	t	f	s
1	2	3	4	5	6	7
8	9	10	11	12	13	14
15	16	17	18	19	20	21
22	23	24	25	26	27	28
29	30					

May

s	m	t	w	t	f	s
		1	2	3	4	5
6	7	8	9	10	11	12
13	14	15	16	17	18	19
20	21	22	23	24	25	26
27	28	29	30	31		

June

s	m	t	w	t	f	s
					1	2
3	4	5	6	7	8	9
10	11	12	13	14	15	16
17	18	19	20	21	22	23
24	25	26	27	28	29	30

July

s	m	t	w	t	f	s
1	2	3	4	5	6	7
8	9	10	11	12	13	14
15	16	17	18	19	20	21
22	23	24	25	26	27	28
29	30	31				

August

s	m	t	w	t	f	s
			1	2	3	4
5	6	7	8	9	10	11
12	13	14	15	16	17	18
19	20	21	22	23	24	25
26	27	28	29	30	31	

September

s	m	t	w	t	f	s
						1
2	3	4	5	6	7	8
9	10	11	12	13	14	15
16	17	18	19	20	21	22
23	24	25	26	27	28	29
30						

October

s	m	t	w	t	f	s
	1	2	3	4	5	6
7	8	9	10	11	12	13
14	15	16	17	18	19	20
21	22	23	24	25	26	27
28	29	30	31			

November

s	m	t	w	t	f	s
				1	2	3
4	5	6	7	8	9	10
11	12	13	14	15	16	17
18	19	20	21	22	23	24
25	26	27	28	29	30	

December

s	m	t	w	t	f	s
						1
2	3	4	5	6	7	8
9	10	11	12	13	14	15
16	17	18	19	20	21	22
23	24	25	26	27	28	29
30	31					

January

s	m	t	w	t	f	s
		1	2	3	4	5
6	7	8	9	10	11	12
13	14	15	16	17	18	19
20	21	22	23	24	25	26
27	28	29	30	31		

February

s	m	t	w	t	f	s
					1	2
3	4	5	6	7	8	9
10	11	12	13	14	15	16
17	18	19	20	21	22	23
24	25	26	27	28	29	

March

s	m	t	w	t	f	s
						1
2	3	4	5	6	7	8
9	10	11	12	13	14	15
16	17	18	19	20	21	22
23	24	25	26	27	28	29
30	31					

April

s	m	t	w	t	f	s
		1	2	3	4	5
6	7	8	9	10	11	12
13	14	15	16	17	18	19
20	21	22	23	24	25	26
27	28	29	30			

May

s	m	t	w	t	f	s
				1	2	3
4	5	6	7	8	9	10
11	12	13	14	15	16	17
18	19	20	21	22	23	24
25	26	27	28	29	30	31

June

s	m	t	w	t	f	s
1	2	3	4	5	6	7
8	9	10	11	12	13	14
15	16	17	18	19	20	21
22	23	24	25	26	27	28
29	30					

July

s	m	t	w	t	f	s
		1	2	3	4	5
6	7	8	9	10	11	12
13	14	15	16	17	18	19
20	21	22	23	24	25	26
27	28	29	30	31		

August

s	m	t	w	t	f	s
					1	2
3	4	5	6	7	8	9
10	11	12	13	14	15	16
17	18	19	20	21	22	23
24	25	26	27	28	29	30
31						

September

s	m	t	w	t	f	s
	1	2	3	4	5	6
7	8	9	10	11	12	13
14	15	16	17	18	19	20
21	22	23	24	25	26	27
28	29	30				

October

s	m	t	w	t	f	s
			1	2	3	4
5	6	7	8	9	10	11
12	13	14	15	16	17	18
19	20	21	22	23	24	25
26	27	28	29	30	31	

November

s	m	t	w	t	f	s
						1
2	3	4	5	6	7	8
9	10	11	12	13	14	15
16	17	18	19	20	21	22
23	24	25	26	27	28	29
30						

December

s	m	t	w	t	f	s
	1	2	3	4	5	6
7	8	9	10	11	12	13
14	15	16	17	18	19	20
21	22	23	24	25	26	27
28	29	30	31			

January

s	m	t	w	t	f	s
				1	2	3
4	5	6	7	8	9	10
11	12	13	14	15	16	17
18	19	20	21	22	23	24
25	26	27	28	29	30	31

February

s	m	t	w	t	f	s
1	2	3	4	5	6	7
8	9	10	11	12	13	14
15	16	17	18	19	20	21
22	23	24	25	26	27	28

March

s	m	t	w	t	f	s
1	2	3	4	5	6	7
8	9	10	11	12	13	14
15	16	17	18	19	20	21
22	23	24	25	26	27	28
29	30	31				

April

s	m	t	w	t	f	s
			1	2	3	4
5	6	7	8	9	10	11
12	13	14	15	16	17	18
19	20	21	22	23	24	25
26	27	28	29	30		

May

s	m	t	w	t	f	s
					1	2
3	4	5	6	7	8	9
10	11	12	13	14	15	16
17	18	19	20	21	22	23
24	25	26	27	28	29	30
31						

June

s	m	t	w	t	f	s
	1	2	3	4	5	6
7	8	9	10	11	12	13
14	15	16	17	18	19	20
21	22	23	24	25	26	27
28	29	30				

July

s	m	t	w	t	f	s
			1	2	3	4
5	6	7	8	9	10	11
12	13	14	15	16	17	18
19	20	21	22	23	24	25
26	27	28	29	30	31	

August

s	m	t	w	t	f	s
						1
2	3	4	5	6	7	8
9	10	11	12	13	14	15
16	17	18	19	20	21	22
23	24	25	26	27	28	29
30	31					

September

s	m	t	w	t	f	s
		1	2	3	4	5
6	7	8	9	10	11	12
13	14	15	16	17	18	19
20	21	22	23	24	25	26
27	28	29	30			

October

s	m	t	w	t	f	s
				1	2	3
4	5	6	7	8	9	10
11	12	13	14	15	16	17
18	19	20	21	22	23	24
25	26	27	28	29	30	31

November

s	m	t	w	t	f	s
1	2	3	4	5	6	7
8	9	10	11	12	13	14
15	16	17	18	19	20	21
22	23	24	25	26	27	28
29	30					

December

s	m	t	w	t	f	s
		1	2	3	4	5
6	7	8	9	10	11	12
13	14	15	16	17	18	19
20	21	22	23	24	25	26
27	28	29	30	31		

January

s	m	t	w	t	f	s
					1	2
3	4	5	6	7	8	9
10	11	12	13	14	15	16
17	18	19	20	21	22	23
24	25	26	27	28	29	30
31						

February

s	m	t	w	t	f	s
	1	2	3	4	5	6
7	8	9	10	11	12	13
14	15	16	17	18	19	20
21	22	23	24	25	26	27
28						

March

s	m	t	w	t	f	s
	1	2	3	4	5	6
7	8	9	10	11	12	13
14	15	16	17	18	19	20
21	22	23	24	25	26	27
28	29	30	31			

April

s	m	t	w	t	f	s
				1	2	3
4	5	6	7	8	9	10
11	12	13	14	15	16	17
18	19	20	21	22	23	24
25	26	27	28	29	30	

May

s	m	t	w	t	f	s
						1
2	3	4	5	6	7	8
9	10	11	12	13	14	15
16	17	18	19	20	21	22
23	24	25	26	27	28	29
30	31					

June

s	m	t	w	t	f	s
		1	2	3	4	5
6	7	8	9	10	11	12
13	14	15	16	17	18	19
20	21	22	23	24	25	26
27	28	29	30			

July

s	m	t	w	t	f	s
				1	2	3
4	5	6	7	8	9	10
11	12	13	14	15	16	17
18	19	20	21	22	23	24
25	26	27	28	29	30	31

August

s	m	t	w	t	f	s
1	2	3	4	5	6	7
8	9	10	11	12	13	14
15	16	17	18	19	20	21
22	23	24	25	26	27	28
29	30	31				

September

s	m	t	w	t	f	s
			1	2	3	4
5	6	7	8	9	10	11
12	13	14	15	16	17	18
19	20	21	22	23	24	25
26	27	28	29	30		

October

s	m	t	w	t	f	s
					1	2
3	4	5	6	7	8	9
10	11	12	13	14	15	16
17	18	19	20	21	22	23
24	25	26	27	28	29	30
31						

November

s	m	t	w	t	f	s
	1	2	3	4	5	6
7	8	9	10	11	12	13
14	15	16	17	18	19	20
21	22	23	24	25	26	27
28	29	30				

December

s	m	t	w	t	f	s
			1	2	3	4
5	6	7	8	9	10	11
12	13	14	15	16	17	18
19	20	21	22	23	24	25
26	27	28	29	30	31	

January

s	m	t	w	t	f	s
						1
2	3	4	5	6	7	8
9	10	11	12	13	14	15
16	17	18	19	20	21	22
23	24	25	26	27	28	29
30	31					

February

s	m	t	w	t	f	s
		1	2	3	4	5
6	7	8	9	10	11	12
13	14	15	16	17	18	19
20	21	22	23	24	25	26
27	28					

March

s	m	t	w	t	f	s
		1	2	3	4	5
6	7	8	9	10	11	12
13	14	15	16	17	18	19
20	21	22	23	24	25	26
27	28	29	30	31		

April

s	m	t	w	t	f	s
					1	2
3	4	5	6	7	8	9
10	11	12	13	14	15	16
17	18	19	20	21	22	23
24	25	26	27	28	29	30

May

s	m	t	w	t	f	s
1	2	3	4	5	6	7
8	9	10	11	12	13	14
15	16	17	18	19	20	21
22	23	24	25	26	27	28
29	30	31				

June

s	m	t	w	t	f	s
			1	2	3	4
5	6	7	8	9	10	11
12	13	14	15	16	17	18
19	20	21	22	23	24	25
26	27	28	29	30		

July

s	m	t	w	t	f	s
					1	2
3	4	5	6	7	8	9
10	11	12	13	14	15	16
17	18	19	20	21	22	23
24	25	26	27	28	29	30
31						

August

s	m	t	w	t	f	s
	1	2	3	4	5	6
7	8	9	10	11	12	13
14	15	16	17	18	19	20
21	22	23	24	25	26	27
28	29	30	31			

September

s	m	t	w	t	f	s
				1	2	3
4	5	6	7	8	9	10
11	12	13	14	15	16	17
18	19	20	21	22	23	24
25	26	27	28	29	30	

October

s	m	t	w	t	f	s
						1
2	3	4	5	6	7	8
9	10	11	12	13	14	15
16	17	18	19	20	21	22
23	24	25	26	27	28	29
30	31					

November

s	m	t	w	t	f	s
		1	2	3	4	5
6	7	8	9	10	11	12
13	14	15	16	17	18	19
20	21	22	23	24	25	26
27	28	29	30			

December

s	m	t	w	t	f	s
				1	2	3
4	5	6	7	8	9	10
11	12	13	14	15	16	17
18	19	20	21	22	23	24
25	26	27	28	29	30	31

Notes

Expenditure Log

Date	Item	Amount	Budget Category	How Paid (cash, credit, etc.)